A Field Guide

QUILTS WITH AN ANGLE

New Foolproof Grid Method & Easy Strip Cutting
15 Projects with Triangles, Hexagons, Diamonds & More

Sheila Christensen

C&T PUBLISHING

Text copyright © 2019 by Sheila Christensen

Photography and artwork copyright © 2019 by C&T Publishing, Inc.

Publisher: Amy Marson

Creative Director: Gailen Runge

Acquisitions Editor: Roxane Cerda

Managing Editor: Liz Aneloski

Editor: Karla Menaugh

Technical Editor: Debbie Rodgers

Cover/Book Designer: April Mostek

Production Coordinator: Tim Manibusan

Production Editor: Jennifer Warren

Illustrator: Kirstie Pettersen

Photo Assistant: Mai Yong Vang

Style photography by Lucy Glover and Kelly Burgoyne; instructional photography by Mai Yong Vang of C&T Publishing, Inc., unless otherwise noted

Published by C&T Publishing, Inc., P.O. Box 1456, Lafayette, CA 94549

Library of Congress Cataloging-in-Publication Data

Names: Christensen, Sheila, 1960- author.

Title: Quilts with an angle : new foolproof grid method & easy strip cutting - 15 projects with triangles, hexagons, diamonds & more / Sheila Christensen.

Description: Lafayette, California : C&T Publishing, [2019] | Includes bibliographical references and index.

Identifiers: LCCN 2018023348 | ISBN 9781617456411 (soft cover)

Subjects: LCSH: Quilting--Patterns. | Geometry in art.

Classification: LCC TT835 .C485 2019 | DDC 746.46/041--dc23

LC record available at https://lccn.loc.gov/2018023348

Printed in China

10 9 8 7 6 5 4 3 2 1

Dedication

Dedicated to the memory of Helen Elizabeth Boddington, 1957–2017.

Original art by Jenny Boddington

Acknowledgments

I would like to thank the following people for their help in writing this book:

Sue Burnett of Busy Bee Quilt Shop for her longarm quilting.

Noeline Day for her longarm quilting on *Pot of Gold*.

Binding queen Vickye Rhind, who did the binding on all except one of the quilts.

My quilting friends Brenda Hilston and Linda Graham, who give support and critique and always seem to know which one is needed.

Jenny Boddington, illustrator extraordinaire, for her technical help with the design on *Bejewelled* and for general moral support.

My fantastic pattern testers: Sheryl Anicich, Lyn Bell, Noeline Day, Kaye Hamer, Sue Kippen, Helen Malanchak, Adrienne Nelson, Adrianne Reid, Vickye Rhind, Sheila Skene, Wendy Welsh, Sheila Williamson, and Jan Wills.

All the wonderful and inspiring teachers who have generously shared their knowledge as I learned to sew and quilt—including Kathy Doughty, who wrote the foreword for this book. Every class I have taken has added a new dimension to my learning.

My New Zealand quilting sisterhood—including Wairarapa Quilters, Capital Quilters, and Aotearoa Quilters—who are always so inspiring.

Robert Kaufman Fabrics for providing the fabric for *Misty Morning* and *Shadowflower*.

Alex Veronelli of Aurifil Threads for providing the threads for piecing and quilting.

Clover, OLFA, and Creative Grids for supplying tools for the step-by-step photos.

My C&T family.

My customers and students at Quilters' Lane for their continued support. Without them, I would not be able to indulge my passion for designing new patterns.

And finally my wonderful husband, Carl, who kept the world turning while I was writing and never complained once.

The world of quilting is nothing without the generosity and support of fellow quilters, and I have never felt it more than right now.

CONTENTS

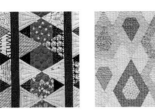
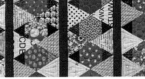

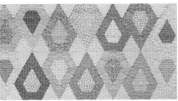

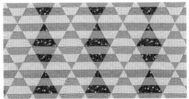

FOREWORD

I met Sheila Christensen several years back when teaching in New Zealand. It was my first visit to that country, and I was overwhelmed by the artistic nature of the quilters living there. Surrounded by wildly beautiful landscapes, isolated from the hustle and bustle of the world ... it seemed a breeding ground for uniqueness and uninhibited creativity. The wonder of the place and people has stayed with me.

At that time, Sheila was about to embark on her new adventure: the patchwork shop. I could tell by the light in her eyes, her earnest nature, and her many questions that she was the right type for the job. Open, friendly, eager, and so enthusiastic—these qualities make a great patchwork shop owner! Feeling safe is a good start to making!

Over the years I have watched her progress as she took on one challenge after another, growing in experience and skill. Patchwork shops are the perfect place to fine-tune, expand, and define quilting skills. The sheer volume of working with different quilters and styles lends us an understanding of not only the best products or methods but also the mind-set of a quilter. There is evidence on each page of this book that Sheila has been paying attention.

There are many things to consider when embarking on a quilting project, and it never hurts to stop and review them all. The first thing I noticed is the easy math language and pointers for getting started. It's clear that Sheila's experience has helped her to develop a language that will speak to quilters at the start of their quilting experience as well as to those that are well on their way. In either case, getting started with the right direction makes the process more rewarding. Tools, techniques, fabrics, and designs all work simultaneously together to create unique and beautiful projects to show off!

Making a quilt is a steady balance of technique and vision. A good book not only guides us through the methods of construction but also considers creating space for a variety of approaches to style and taste. A good book can open the mind to new ways of seeing what we already know. Any one of the many projects combined with the outlined color strategies, the 60° shapes, and your stash will help you achieve the results that you desire.

Enjoy your travels through these wonderful shapes with Sheila!

Kathy Doughty is a self-taught quilter, fabric designer, and author. She designs fabrics for FreeSpirit Fabrics and is the owner of Material Obsession, a patchwork shop in Sydney, Australia.

INTRODUCTION

One of the things I love about quilting is that the design possibilities are endless. Whenever one design is completed, ideas for a myriad of others take its place. Ideas build on previous patterns from our quilting heritage and from different cultures, art, and architecture.

Each quilting technique has its own language. If you use squares and rectangles, you will understand what a half-square triangle is and how to cut a quarter-square triangle. You can find charts that tell you what size quarter-square triangle to cut to achieve a certain size of square. If you are an English paper-piecing aficionado, you understand that you can put together pieces with edges of equal sizes. These rules allow you to try out new ideas within the technique that you are most comfortable with.

In writing this book, I have tried to develop a set of techniques and a language that will allow quilters to play in a new sandbox—the 60° shape. Although

these shapes have been widely used in quilts, there has never been a standard way of measuring for rotary cutting and machine piecing these shapes. Quilt designs based on a 60° grid can look very complex, but once they are broken down into blocks, you will see how easy it is to put them together.

When designing my blocks, I wanted to make sure that they could easily be sewn using straightforward rotary-cutting and machine-piecing techniques. All of the quilts in this book can be made by anyone who is used to cutting and sewing squares, rectangles, and half-square triangles. You will soon be making blocks and turning them into amazing quilts with an angle!

You can generate all sorts of interesting patterns with different placements of these blocks. Just like combining square-shaped blocks, the possibilities are endless.

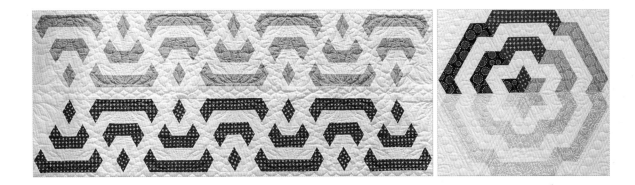

Triangular Grids

The key to creating my blocks was to use a grid made up of triangles. Just as a square grid can be broken down into squares, rectangles, half-square triangles, and so on to create thousands of traditional blocks, a triangular grid can be combined into triangles, diamonds, parallelograms, trapezoids, hexagons, and jewels.

The blocks in this book are mostly based on a sixteen-patch or a thirty-six–patch triangular grid.

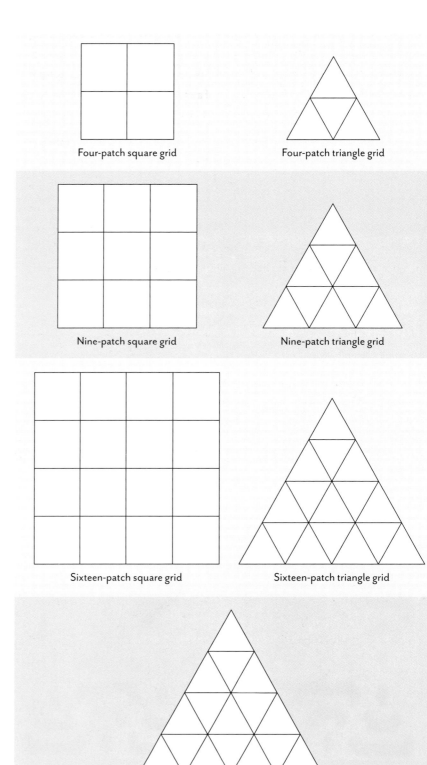

Four-patch square grid

Four-patch triangle grid

Nine-patch square grid

Nine-patch triangle grid

Sixteen-patch square grid

Sixteen-patch triangle grid

Thirty-six–patch triangle grid

Defining Patch Sizes

The width of an equilateral triangle—a 60° triangle—is not the same as its height. To make the patterns easy to understand, I refer to the finished height of a block or a shape throughout the book. For example, an 8″ finished triangle starts out as 8½″ high unfinished when cut using my strip method and a triangle ruler. (The width is approximately 9¼″ finished and 9⅞″ unfinished, but if you use a triangle ruler or follow the 60° lines on your ruler for cutting, you don't have to worry about this.)

The Blocks

Most of the projects in this book are based on one of six triangle-shaped blocks that I have created, from very basic (like Simply Triangles) to a little more complex (like Tie Me in Knots). The blocks are either 8″ or 12″ finished height, but the techniques can be applied to any size of block.

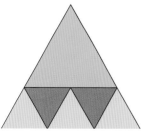

Simply Triangles block (page 39)

Peak block (page 62)

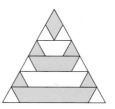

Stack the Dishes block (page 80)

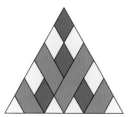

Tie Me in Knots block (page 97)

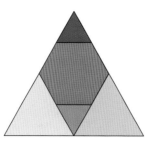

Tri-Hex block (page 121)

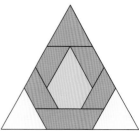

Petal block (page 139)

Why Measure by Height?

If you have done any English paper piecing, you may be used to measuring pieces along their edges. This makes sense when you are joining pieces by hand and when any shape can be made to match any other along the seam.

For my 60° patchwork system, measuring by height makes it simple to cut all of the pieces from standard-size strips using a rotary cutter and ruler. Triangle rulers are marked with lines that are easy measurements from the tip of the ruler, making it straightforward to cut any of the pieces in this book.

Quilt Settings

I have used two different types of setting designs to make very different quilts from the same block. In the straight setting, the blocks are set in rows. In the kaleidoscope setting, the tops of all the blocks point in toward the middle. There is no difference in the method of construction, as the triangle blocks are always sewn together in rows; it is how the blocks are oriented that creates the alternative patterns.

Take a simple block like this:

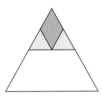

Here's one way to put it into a straight setting.

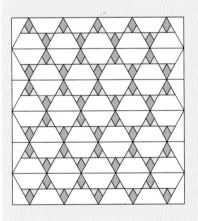

Here's an alternative straight setting.

And here is the same block put into a kaleidoscope setting.

What a difference!

I am having so much fun with these designs, and I'm sure that the quilts in this book are just the beginning of my journey to explore the triangle grid and all the amazing quilts that can be created from them. Join me on this exciting adventure!

Mirror Mirror (page 63) and *Court and Spark* (page 68)

Watling Street (page 123) and *Bliss* (page 128)

GETTING STARTED

TOOLS

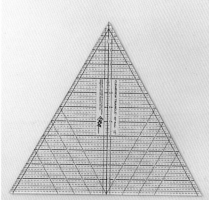

To get started with 60° shapes, you will need a basic set of tools used for standard patchwork. If you add a 60° triangle ruler, cutting will be much faster and easier.

Rulers

You will need a 6˝ × 24˝ ruler (or similar size). Useful additions to your ruler collection are a 6˝ × 12˝ rectangle, 6˝ × 6˝ square, and 12½˝ × 12½˝ square.

Cutting the shapes will be easier if you also have a 60° triangle ruler that is at least 8˝ in height—preferably 12˝. There are various brands available, but ensure that your ruler measures the height of the triangles and not the sides. If you can, add a smaller triangle ruler, as this is easier to handle when cutting smaller pieces.

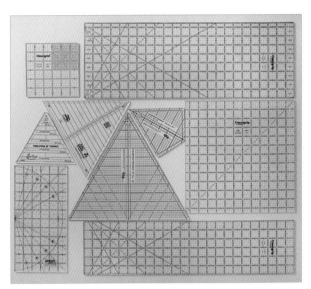

There are many types of 60° rulers on the market to add to your collection of straight rulers.

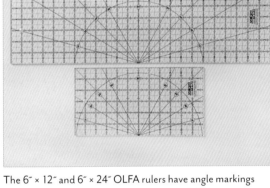

The 6˝ × 12˝ and 6˝ × 24˝ OLFA rulers have angle markings running from the center. I find this very useful for trimming 60° blocks.

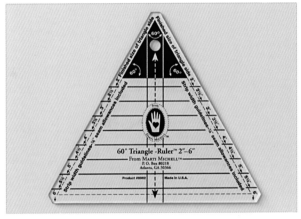

These triangles measure along the edge and are designed for English paper piecing. They will not work for the patterns in this book.

More About Triangle Rulers

It is very easy to cut 60° shapes from strips using triangle rulers, and there are many different triangle rulers on the market. You will need one where the measurements run from top to bottom and indicate the height of the triangle you are cutting. Of those, there are two types—point tip and blunt tip.

Point-tip rulers: The measurements on these rulers start at the very tip of the ruler. Brands include Clearview Triangle (by C&T Publishing), Matilda's Own, and SewEasy.

The instructions that come with these rulers will tell you to cut strips ¾˝ wider than the finished height of the piece you wish to cut. But I have found that you can easily cut shapes from the same strip size you would use for a blunt-tip ruler by letting the top ¼˝ of the point-tip ruler overhang the strip. You still use the height + ¾˝ line to determine where to cut, but you end up with a blunt-tip triangle exactly the same size as one cut with a blunt-tip ruler.

Point-tip ruler

Blunt-tip rulers: The measurements start at the top of the ruler, which doesn't include the top ¼˝ of the triangle tip. The instructions for these rulers will tell you to add ½˝ to the finished height of the piece you wish to cut. These include Creative Grids and Quilt in a Day rulers.

You can use either type of triangle ruler in the lessons and projects in this book, using exactly the same strip width for either ruler. The difference is which ruler line you will use to cut the shape.

If in doubt, use the patterns (page 38) to check which line to use on your ruler. Another option is to photocopy the pattern, cut it out, and stick it to the bottom of your triangle ruler. I have also included cutting directions for using the 60° line on a straight ruler if you prefer this method.

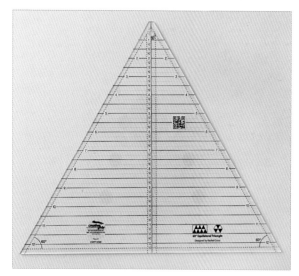

Blunt-tip ruler

Other Piecing Tools for 60° Shapes

I have a collection of additional tools in my studio that I would not be without when piecing 60° shapes.

Corner Cut 60—2-in-1 Sewing Tool   This tool by C&T Publishing is really useful for cutting off the tips of shapes, which helps them fit together in a breeze.

Finger-presser   With the Roll & Press (by Clover), you can press all of your seams open without having to get up and press each piece with an iron before attaching the next. You can also use a bamboo or plastic finger-presser or even a small wallpaper seam roller.

Sharp snips or small scissors   These are great for snipping off any tips that you missed when cutting and for cutting apart chain piecing.

Extrafine patchwork pins   Clover's fine glass-head patchwork pins and flower-head pins slip through fabric easily without distorting the seams.

Mary Ellen's Best Press, Flatter (by Soak), or similar starch alternative   Starch alternative is your best friend when dealing with very small pieces. It helps keep bias edges under control.

Thread

I like to use a cotton thread with my cotton fabric, and Aurifil 50 weight is my thread of choice for piecing. It is fine and strong and produces very little lint. A bonus of using this finer thread is that you don't have to change the bobbin as often and seams sit flatter.

Use a neutral color for piecing. Gray or cream will blend in much better than white or black.

For quilting, Aurifil has some beautiful variegated colors as well as plains. Use a 50-weight thread, or go a little thicker with a 40-weight thread. These are available on cones for longarm quilters.

It's nice to add hand quilting in big stitches on your quilts. Use either Aurifil 12 weight, Wonderfil Eleganza, or Valdani perle cotton #8 or #12.

CHOOSING
FABRICS

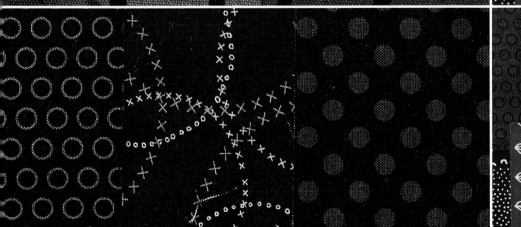

The best fabric for patchwork is 100% cotton. Man-made fibers cannot take the heat that is needed for pressing seams and will not hold their shape. Buying from your local quilt shop or trusted online retailer will ensure you get the best-quality fabric that will be a pleasure to work with and last a lifetime. Proper quilting cottons are also resistant to dyes running and fading. There is really no substitute for seeing and feeling the fabric, so do try to buy in person if you can.

One of the most common statements I get from quilters coming into my shop is "I'm no good with color." I'm not sure why so many people think they can't choose fabrics. Maybe it is because there are so many different combinations that work, and we are always comparing ourselves to our neighbor, who may have completely different tastes. The good news is that everyone can choose colors. There are no rules about what is right and wrong—just guidelines that can help if you are feeling stuck.

Color Terms

Here are some useful terms for describing colors.

Hue: This is what we usually think of when we talk about color—red, green, blue, aqua, and so on.

Value: The relative lightness or darkness of a color.

Saturation or intensity: How strong a color is. A very bright color is saturated or intense.

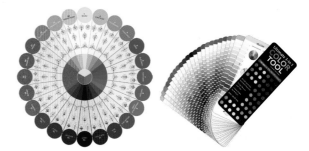

Joen Wolfrom's Studio Color Wheel and Ultimate 3-in-1 Color Tool (by C&T Publishing) are excellent tools for learning about and using colors.

Creating Contrast

A high level of contrast means you can clearly see a defining line between two fabrics. Contrast can be light versus dark, bright versus dull, or contrasting hues (such as red versus green). In patchwork you can also use pattern as a way of creating contrast—for example, by putting a spot next to a plain fabric.

Strategies for Choosing Colors

First, Choose What You Love

The most reliable way of choosing fabrics is to start by finding something that really grabs your attention and that you love, then adding to it. Don't worry if you feel like you are always staying in your comfort zone. You can push the boundaries a little bit using the strategies I am going to give you; eventually you may find you are moving into new areas and surprise yourself.

Strategy One: Make a Rainbow

In *Caravan* (page 41) and *After the Storm* (page 48), I used a collection of fabric that was designed around the color wheel. Try organizing your stash around the color wheel. You probably have some parts of the wheel where you have lots of fabrics and other places with not much. That's okay. A rainbow quilt doesn't need to include every color.

Rainbow quilts rely on hue as a way of selecting fabrics. You can use one of the great color tools by Joen Wolfrom to help you—this is really useful when you get to fine details such as sorting turquoise from aqua and deciding where violet goes in relation to purple. Also remember the child-hood rhyme that tells you how the rainbow flows: "**R**ichard (red) **o**f (orange) **Y**ork (yellow) **g**ave (green) **b**attle (blue) **i**n (indigo) **v**ain (violet)."

Use vibrant, intense colors; soft and pretty colors; or more traditionally toned and grayed colors (what I call "country colors"). If you stay within the same tonal value (bright versus grayed out), you can't go wrong.

I used Jasmine by Valori Wells for a rainbow effect.

Strategy Two: Create a Bold and Dynamic Effect Using Contrasting Values

Mirror Mirror (page 63) and *Court and Spark* (page 68) show how using dramatically different values creates a bold statement.

To make the designs stand out, pay attention to contrast. You can create contrast by using value, such as having light and dark fabrics next to each other. If you have a high level of contrast, you will create a bold, dramatic effect. A lower level of contrast is more calming.

Black and white, red and white, or blue and white are classic combinations. Brown and cream would be a softer alternative.

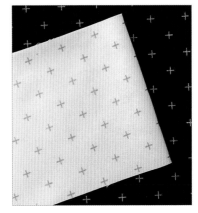

Create a dramatic effect with a high level of contrast.

Strategy Three: Change Your Background Color

Misty Morning (page 82) and *Shadowflower* (page 87) are rainbow quilts, but they look quite different from *Caravan* (page 41) and *After the Storm* (page 48). Changing the background color can create a very different look—from vibrant and striking when paired with a dark background to soft and pretty against a crisp white.

A white background gives a soft and pretty effect.

Darker backgrounds make a striking difference.

Strategy Four: Create a Calm and Organized Look

Using hues that are next to each other on the color wheel is called a *harmonious color scheme*. The fabrics look organized and classic. In *Bejewelled* (page 100) and *Cosmic Rays* (page 106), I started with a pretty navy floral by Cotton + Steel and paired it with one of their blenders in teal, close to blue on the color wheel. Adding the light aqua print brings some depth, and the background fabrics are all low-volume prints.

Blue and green are close on the color wheel.

Strategy Five: Controlled Scrappy

This is probably my favorite strategy for choosing colors. In *Watling Street* (page 123) and *Bliss* (page 128), I used a very controlled level of scrappiness. Just one *hue*, or color, is contrasted against a low-volume background, with darks and lights creating lots of interest and highlighting the pattern.

This collection of lipstick reds creates more interest than using one single fabric.

Strategy Six: Contrasting Intensity or Hue

Both *Patisserie* (page 141) and *Apple Blossom Time* (page 146) are firmly in the sweet and pretty camp. Using a variety of coral-colored prints that were quite close together in *Apple Blossom Time* is very calming, but the quilt needed a bit of zing. The yellow is a contrast of color intensity—it is fairly close to coral on the color wheel but more saturated in color and therefore pops out and adds interest.

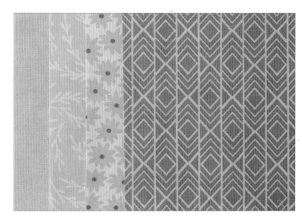

Add some zing with yellow.

For *Patisserie*, I used contrasting colors on opposite sides of the color wheel to add interest. The overall effect is still fairly soft, as the colors are pastel tints.

Slice of Heaven (page 166) uses blue and yellow, opposite colors on the wheel. Take hints from the feature fabrics you select. (Fabric designers are experts at combining colors, so harness their knowledge!) The blue floral print includes yellow lemons, so this made choosing the yellow fabric an easy task.

WHAT IS A LOW-VOLUME PRINT?

Low-volume prints are low in contrast levels and provide an interesting look that is more exciting that having one single background fabric. Build up your collection of low volumes and you will always have something to use as a scrappy background without worrying about having exactly the right quantity of a single fabric.

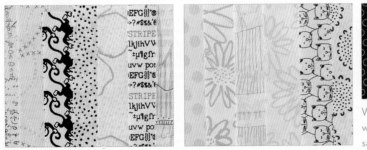

Some fun low-volume prints include color, not just neutrals.

While most people think of light prints when they talk about low volume, the same concept can work for a dark—or any color—background.

60° PATCHWORK BASICS

These are some basic techniques that I teach to my beginning quilters. Even if you have been quilting for a long time, it is always great to take classes and learn how other people do things. I am always learning new techniques and tips to make my life easier.

Fabric Care

Your fabric may have come straight from the bolt in the shop, as a fat quarter, or as an odd-shaped piece from your stash. I don't wash my fabric before sewing, but you can if you want. If you have prewashed, a spray of Mary Ellen's Best Press or other starch alternative will give the fabric the crisp feel that it may have lost in washing. It is always good to press before you start to cut.

Straight Grain

If your fabric is off the bolt or a fat quarter, it is easy to see where the straight grain lies.

The grain runs perpendicular and parallel to the selvage. It will not stretch much if pulled in either direction.

If you pull the fabric on the bias, you will see that there is much more stretch.

In all 60° patchwork, at least two edges of each shape will be cut partly on the bias. This means it is important to take a bit of extra care when handling these pieces and especially when using the iron.

Cutting Strips

Cutting strips is the first step in cutting all of the shapes in this book.

Accurate cutting is just as important as accurate piecing to achieving a good result. Always use the quilting ruler to measure your strips, as cutting mats are not accurate enough for measuring.

1. Start with a good, sharp blade in your rotary cutter. I change mine with each project.

2. Place the fabric on the cutting mat with the selvage toward you. I keep my fabric folded as it came off the bolt and bring this fold toward me. Place the fold even with the selvage. This makes a short distance for the rotary cutter to travel and minimizes the possibility of slipping.

> **NOTE: SAFETY FIRST**
> *Rotary cutter blades are extremely sharp. Every time you cut, replace the safety guide before you put the cutter down.*

Right-Handed Cutting

1. Place the ruler on the right-hand side of the fabric and line up with the fold. Use the rotary cutter to square off the edge of the fabric. **FIG. A**

2. Turn either the mat or the fabric so the squared-off edge is on your left.

For a 2½˝ strip, place a straight quilting ruler with the 2½˝ line on the edge of the fabric. **FIG. B**

3. Cut. **FIG. C**

4. Continue cutting strips by moving the ruler along onto the cut edge.

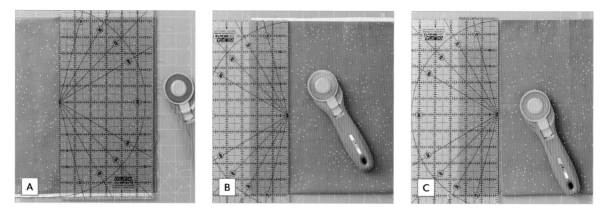

Left-Handed Cutting

1. Place the ruler on the left-hand side of the fabric and line up with the fold. Use the rotary cutter to square off the edge of the fabric. **FIG. D**

2. Turn either the mat or the fabric so the squared-off edge is on your right. **FIG. E**

For a 2½˝ strip, place a straight quilting ruler with the 2½˝ line on the edge of the fabric. Cut.

3. Continue cutting strips by moving the ruler along onto the cut edge.

Follow each lesson to learn how to cut triangles, trapezoids, diamonds, parallelograms, hexagons, and jewels from width-of-fabric strips.

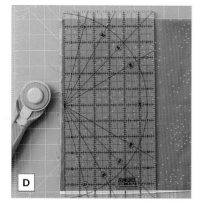
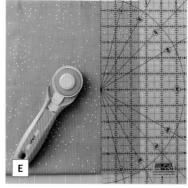

Seams

All seams are a *scant ¼˝*. *Scant* means one or two thread widths less than ¼˝.

The math of sewing two seams on either side of a 2½˝ piece means the end result should measure 2˝. However, when you press your seams, one or two threads are taken up in the fold. That is why the seams need to be slightly less than ¼˝.

To achieve a perfect seam width, there are special feet available for most sewing machines. It is still necessary to practice sewing the seams. Some machines have a specific needle-position setting for ¼˝ piecing. Read the manual to see if you have this facility on your machine.

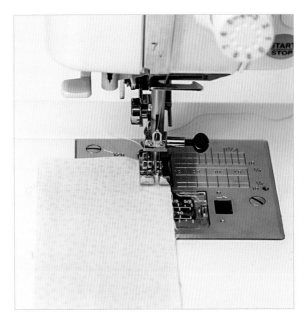

HOW TO CHECK THE SEAM WIDTH

This is one of the simple fixes that can make your quilting life much easier and will pay dividends when it comes to joining blocks.

Keep practicing ¼˝ seams until you are confident that you have the right setup for your own machine.

1. Cut 3 pieces of fabric exactly 2½˝ × 6˝.

2. Sew 2 of the pieces together with a scant ¼˝ seam. Press the seam open.

3. Sew the third piece to the second piece. Press open. Check that you do not press in any pleats and that your seams lie flat.

4. Using a quilting ruler, measure the resulting width of the center strip. This should be exactly 2˝.

If the center strip is less than 2˝, the seams are too wide.

If the center strip is more than 2˝, the seams are too narrow.

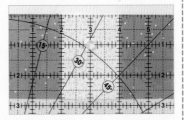

Sewing 60° Seams

The seams in 60° patchwork are a little different to match and trim than the seams in regular patchwork, but the principles are the same. It is still important to keep a ¼˝ seam allowance and press the seams well.

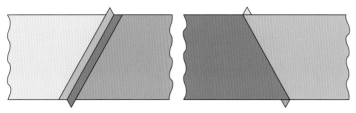

A simple 60° seam, front and back view (seams pressed open).
This is without any of the tips trimmed off.

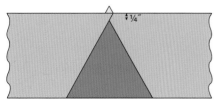

When two seams cross, the intersection should lie ¼˝ from the edge.

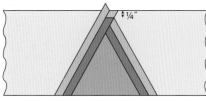

Note where you can see the seam between the blue and gray on the back. If your needle goes precisely through this seam when joining to another piece, you will achieve perfect points.

The seam intersections can be used to line up pieces when joining. Either pinch the pieces together and peek into the seam to make sure they match, or push a pin through both points.

Notice how the tip from the back triangle is visible from the front and its edge lines up with the edge of the front seam. This can help you line up many of your 60° seams. It can sometimes be helpful to leave the tips on sewn pieces.

Trimming Corners

Once you have made a few blocks, you will work out your own preferred practices for when to trim and when not to trim the corners. If you don't trim the corners before piecing, make sure you trim them afterward, as this will reduce bulk in the seams.

Trimming the tips of the shapes with a Corner Cut 60—2-in-1 Sewing Tool (page 16) or the tip of your ruler can help make everything slot into place, especially when you first start.

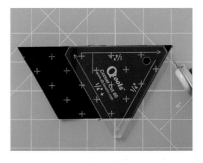

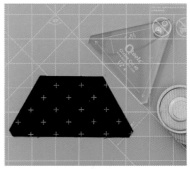

Chain Piecing

When you have a pile of small pieces to sew, chain piecing is a quick method to get the job done.

I use a leader when I start a chain. Once you complete a set of units, feed the leader back in and "park" the needle in it.

Chain piecing means sewing one unit after another. Keep feeding each of the pieces in, and when you have finished, you will have what looks like bunting. Snip the units apart once they are sewn.

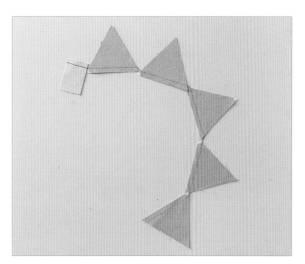

TIP **Using a Leader**

Use a small piece of fabric as a leader. Stitch to the edge of this piece and leave it in place before feeding in your next piece. This saves thread and stops the tips of triangles from being pushed down into the bobbin case area.

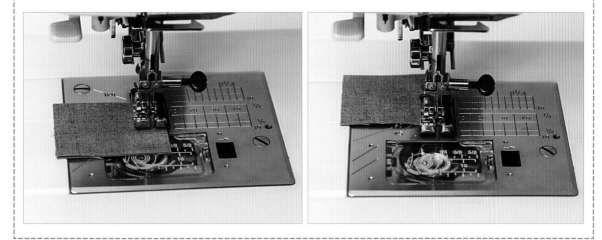

Pressing

After sewing seams, always press well. For 60° piecing, I press my seams open; but when joining blocks and rows, I often press to one side. Make sure to *press* rather than *iron*. Press downward and do not twist the iron to and fro, as this can stretch the fabric. This is particularly important for triangles because there are many bias edges in the pieces. I use my Clover Roll & Press while assembling blocks and then take the completed block to the iron to give it a final press.

LESSON ONE:
60° TRIANGLE

60° TRIANGLE BASICS

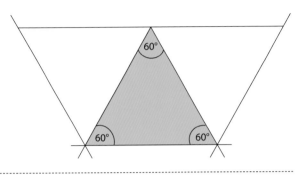

In Perfect Balance

With three equal sides and three equal angles, equilateral triangles are like the squares of 60° patchwork. They are the basic building blocks for all of the shapes in this book.

On the Grid

Triangles are defined by their finished height when sewn. They also can be thought of in terms of the space they occupy on a triangle grid.

On a 1″ grid, a 2″ triangle is 2 grid units high × 2 grid units wide and contains 4 grid spaces.

A 4″ finished height triangle is 4 grid units high × 4 grid units wide and contains 16 grid spaces.

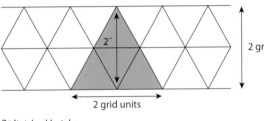

2″ finished height

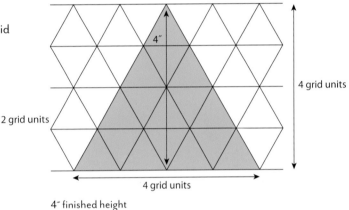

4″ finished height

How Triangle Sizes Are Defined

In my system, triangles are defined by their finished height when sewn and not the width. Because the angle is always the same, the width will take care of itself.

The sides of equilateral triangles are longer than the height of the triangle, so a 2″ finished height triangle is wider than 2″. (The width is approximately 2⁵⁄₁₆″ finished and 3³⁄₁₆″ unfinished, but if you use a triangle ruler for cutting, you don't have to worry about this.)

In the cutting lists for the projects, you will see the width of the unfinished triangle base in the Cut Size column. Most of the time you will not need to use this figure while cutting, whether you use a triangle ruler or a straight ruler with 60° lines.

TYPES OF RULERS

Triangle rulers are not standard across the industry. For cutting triangles, it is important to know which ruler type you are using. For both types of triangle rulers, use the same size of fabric strip, but choose a different cutting line depending on the ruler. Instructions are given for both types. More information on rulers is found in Tools (page 13).

- Point-tip rulers include the tip of the triangle in the measurement. To find the ruler line to use, add ¾˝ to the finished height of the triangle.

- Blunt-tip rulers have a truncated tip, and measurements start from there. To find the ruler line to use, add ½˝ to the finished height of the triangle.

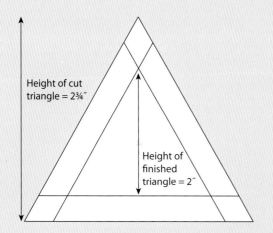

Height of cut triangle = 2¾˝

Height of finished triangle = 2˝

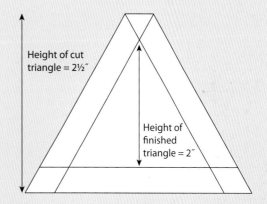

Height of cut triangle = 2½˝

Height of finished triangle = 2˝

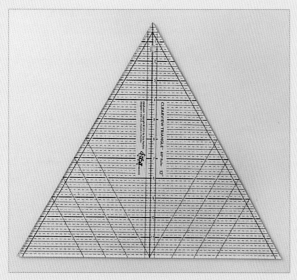

Point tip, such as the Clearview Triangle ruler by C&T Publishing

Blunt tip, such as the 60° Equilateral Triangle ruler by Creative Grids

Cutting 60° Triangles

Cutting Triangles with a Triangle Ruler

1. Start by cutting a strip of fabric ½˝ wider than the finished height of the triangle. For a 2˝ finished height triangle, cut a 2½˝ strip. This allows for ¼˝ seam allowances on the top and bottom. See Cutting Strips (page 23).

> **NOTE: LEFT-HANDED CUTTING**
>
> *If you are left-handed like me, you will cut from the right-hand end of the strips. Turn the book upside down to make it easier to understand the cutting photos.*

2. If you are using a point-tip ruler: Place the ruler with the 2¾˝ line on the bottom of the fabric strip. Cut on both sides of the ruler. Note that the tip of the ruler extends past the top of the fabric strip. **FIG. A**

If you are using a blunt-tip ruler: Place the ruler with the 2½˝ line on the bottom of the fabric strip. Cut on both sides of the ruler. Note that the tip of the ruler lines up with the top of the fabric strip. **FIG. B**

3. Continue cutting more triangles by rotating the ruler and cutting again. You can also flip the fabric over if it is easier than moving the ruler. Once you have practiced cutting triangles, you can cut more than 1 layer of fabric at a time. **FIG. C**

> **TIP** **60° Triangle Cutting Tip**
>
> If you are cutting lots of triangles the same, you can use ruler tape or masking tape on the ruler line you are using to save from making mistakes.
>
>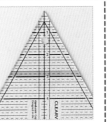

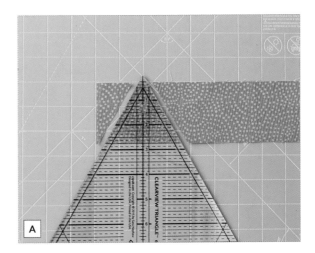

A

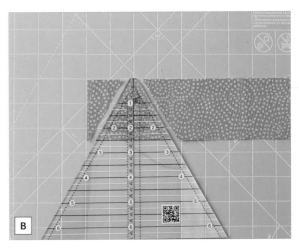

B

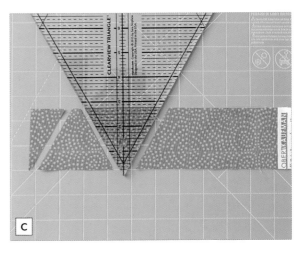

C

Quick Reference: Cutting 60° Triangles with Triangle Rulers

FINISHED HEIGHT	STRIP WIDTH	POINT-TIP RULER LINE	BLUNT-TIP RULER LINE
2″	2½″	2¾″	2½″
4″	4½″	4¾″	4½″
6″	6½″	6¾″	6½″
8″	8½″	8¾″	8½″
10″	10½″	10¾″	10½″
12″	12½″	Use a 12¾″ strip and see straight-ruler cutting instructions below.	12½″

Cutting Triangles with a Straight Ruler

Triangle rulers make it easy to cut accurate triangle shapes. But if you do not have a triangle ruler, you can still cut triangles! In fact, some of the patterns include triangles that are larger than most triangle rulers; you will need to use a straight ruler with 60° lines to cut these.

Start with a strip that is ¾″ wider than the finished height of the triangle. To cut a triangle with a straight ruler, use the 60° markings on the ruler.

1. Align one of the 60° lines of the ruler with the top edge of the strip. Make a cut. **FIG. D**

2. Rotate the ruler to align the other 60° line with the top edge of the strip. Make a cut. Your triangles will have pointed tips. **FIG. E**

3. To cut more triangles from the strip, continue to move the ruler down the strip, switching back and forth from the first 60° ruler line to the second.

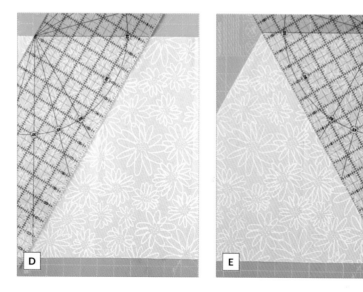

Cutting Triangles Larger than the Ruler

If you have a triangle ruler (either style) but want to cut a triangle bigger than the ruler, you can use it to line up the straight ruler and cut. Start with a fabric strip that is ¾″ wider than the finished height.

1. Line up the triangle ruler and straight ruler. **FIG. A**

2. Remove the triangle ruler and cut. **FIG. B**

3. Turn the triangle ruler and line up with the top edge of the fabric. Place the straight ruler alongside. **FIG. C**

4. Remove the triangle ruler and cut. **FIG. D**

5. Continue along the strip in the same way.

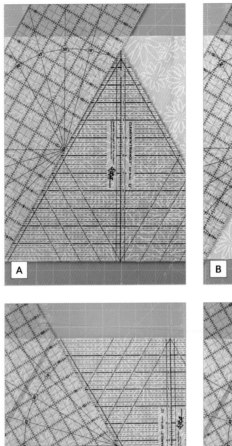

A

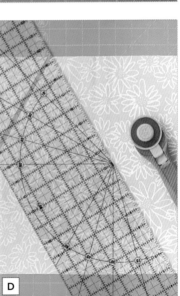

B

C

D

Quick Reference: Cutting 60° Triangles with Straight Rulers

Remember, 60° triangles are always wider than they are tall. You won't need to use the length of the triangle base to cut triangles, but it can be helpful to know, so I've listed it here. The exact base measurements (used for straight-ruler cutting) would fall at odd places along the inch marker; I've rounded them to the closest $\frac{1}{16}''$.

FINISHED HEIGHT	STRIP WIDTH	APPROXIMATE LENGTH OF TRIANGLE BASE
1″	1¾″	2″
2″	2¾″	3³⁄₁₆″
3″	3¾″	4⅜″
4″	4¾″	5½″
5″	5¾″	6¹¹⁄₁₆″
6″	6¾″	7¹³⁄₁₆″
7″	7¾″	9″
8″	8¾″	10⅛″
9″	9¾″	11⁵⁄₁₆″
10″	10¾″	12⁷⁄₁₆″
11″	11¾″	13⅝″
12″	12¾″	14¾″
13″	13¾″	15⅞″
14″	14¾″	17¹⁄₁₆″
15″	15¾″	18³⁄₁₆″
16″	16¾″	19⅜″
17″	17¾″	20½″
18″	18¾″	21¹¹⁄₁₆″
19″	19¾″	22¹³⁄₁₆″
20″	20¾″	24″

TIP **Using the Optional Patterns**

If you are not sure how to line up your ruler, you can use a pattern (page 38) for the smaller sizes to check the size.

Piecing 60° Triangles

1. Lay the triangles side by side with the straight grain running from top to bottom. **FIG. A**

2. Pick up the right-hand triangle and place it on top of the other triangle with right sides together. Line up the pieces carefully. Because the tips of the triangles are cut off, you will see the corner of the bottom triangle on the right-hand side. **FIG. B**

3. Sew a ¼˝ seam. Note how this ends where the 2 triangle corners cross. **FIG. C**

4. Press the seam open. **FIG. D**

5. *Optional:* Trim off the tips. Doing this helps to reduce bulk in the seams so that your work will stay flat. **FIG. E**

6. Add another triangle. **FIG. F**

7. Once you have sewn 3 triangles together, the seams should cross ¼˝ from the raw edge. **FIGS. G & H**

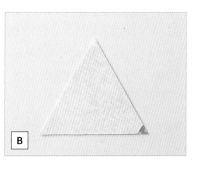

A

B

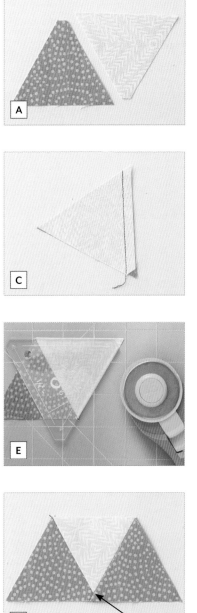

C

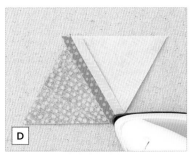

D

E

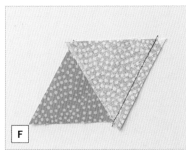

F

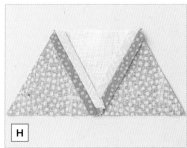

G

Seams cross ¼˝ from raw edge.

H

Note where the seams are lined up on the reverse.

Cutting Half-Triangles

In the projects, I use 30° triangles—which I call *half-triangles*—to square up blocks or quilt edges. After all, 30 + 60 = 90, and 90° is a square corner. To cut these shapes, start with a rectangle. I will give you the size in the patterns, and you can refer to the chart (below) for other sizes. Cut the rectangle in half diagonally to make 2 half-triangles, both slanted in the same direction. Most of the time, you will have to cut half of the rectangles in one direction and the other half in the opposite direction so you have equal numbers of half-triangles slanted in each direction.

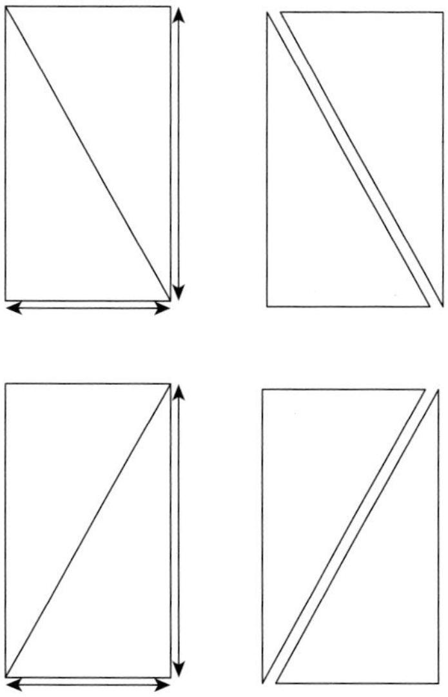

Quick Reference: Cutting Half-Triangles

To cut half-triangles, start with a rectangle. Cut it in half diagonally to get 2 half-triangles angled in the same direction.

TIP Most rulers do not have 1/16″ markings. 1/16″ is half of 1/8″. For example, 3/16″ is halfway between 1/8″ and 1/4″.

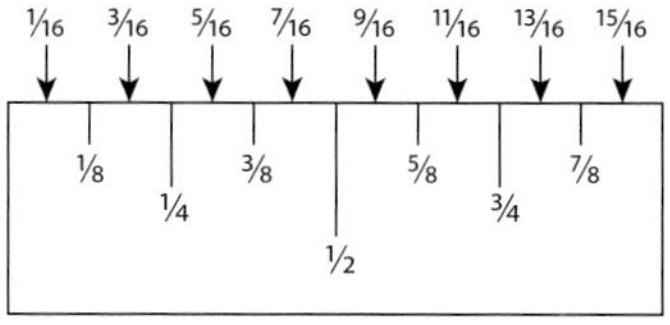

FINISHED HEIGHT	SIZE OF RECTANGLE	FINISHED HEIGHT	SIZE OF RECTANGLE
1″	2 3/16″ × 1 1/4″	11″	12 3/16″ × 7 1/16″
2″	3 3/16″ × 1 13/16″	12″	13 3/16″ × 7 5/8″
3″	4 3/16″ × 2 7/16″	13″	14 3/16″ × 8 3/16″
4″	5 3/16″ × 3″	14″	15 3/16″ × 8 13/16″
5″	6 3/16″ × 3 9/16″	15″	16 3/16″ × 9 3/8″
6″	7 3/16″ × 4 1/8″	16″	17 3/16″ × 9 15/16″
7″	8 3/16″ × 4 3/4″	17″	18 3/16″ × 10 1/2″
8″	9 3/16″ × 5 5/16″	18″	19 3/16″ × 11 1/16″
9″	10 3/16″ × 5 7/8″	19″	20 3/16″ × 11 5/8″
10″	11 3/16″ × 6 7/16″	20″	21 3/16″ × 12 1/4″

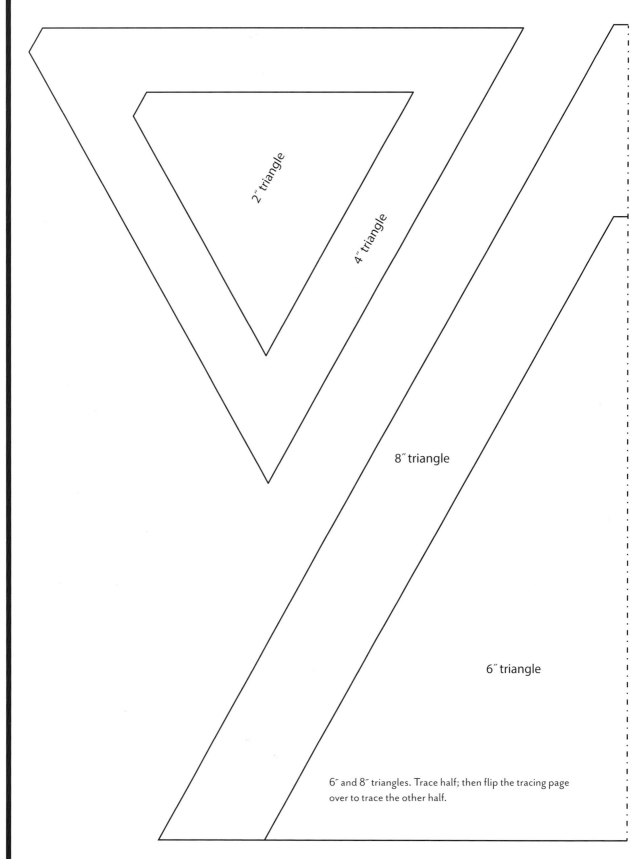

2˝ triangle

4˝ triangle

8˝ triangle

6˝ triangle

6˝ and 8˝ triangles. Trace half; then flip the tracing page over to trace the other half.

Simply Triangles Block

FINISHED BLOCK HEIGHT: 12˝

Learn how to make this simple block, which is used in *Caravan* and *After the Storm*.

MATERIALS

Fabric 1 (dark blue): 8½˝ × half width of fabric strip (8¾˝ × half width of fabric if cutting with a straight ruler) for the 8˝ finished height triangle

Fabric 2 (gray): 4½˝ × half width of fabric strip (4¾˝ × half width of fabric if cutting with a straight ruler) for the 4˝ finished height triangles

Fabric 3 (blue with camels): 4½˝ × half width of fabric strip (4¾˝ × half width of fabric if cutting with a straight ruler) for the 4˝ finished height triangles

CUTTING

For more detailed cutting instructions, see Cutting 60° Triangles (page 32).

SHAPE	CUT SIZE	FIRST, CUT FABRIC STRIPS:	SUBCUT FROM STRIPS:
Fabric 1			
△ 8˝ triangle	8½˝ tall, 10⅛˝ base	1 strip 8½˝* × half width of fabric	1 triangle
Fabric 2			
△ 4˝ triangle	4½˝ tall, 5½˝ base	1 strip 4½˝* × half width of fabric	2 triangles
Fabric 3			
△ 4˝ triangle	4½˝ tall, 5½˝ base	1 strip 4½˝* × half width of fabric	3 triangles. For directional fabric, see note below.

If using a straight ruler to cut the triangles, start with a strip ¼˝ wider than the size listed. The cut size of your triangle will be ¼˝ taller than the cut size in the chart.

NOTE *My fabric is directional, and I wanted all of the camels upright, so I moved the ruler along the strip to cut the second and third triangles. If you are using nondirectional fabric, you can rotate the ruler and cut from both sides.*

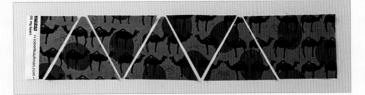

Make the Block

Use scant ¼″ seams.

1. Join the fabric 2 and fabric 3 triangles in a row. Press the seams open. **FIG. A**

2. Pin this row to the fabric 1 triangle. Sew. **FIGS. B & C**

A

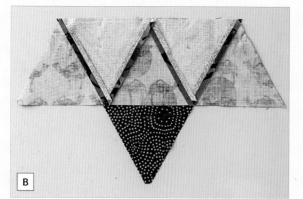

B

C

Note how the seam intersects where the two fabrics meet.

TIP Notice how the tips of the large triangle extend at each end. An alternative is to use a trimming tool and remove these tips to help line up the pieces for sewing

3. Open the block and press. **FIG. D**

I love to play with these blocks in different layouts to see what patterns I can make. In *Caravan*, the blocks are in a straight setting. *After the Storm* uses a kaleidoscope setting, but there are even more ways that you can put these blocks together. Try laying out a few blocks on your design wall, rotating them, and looking at the possibilities!

D

Simply Triangles block

Quilting suggestion for Simply Triangles block

Caravan

FINISHED BLOCK HEIGHT: 12˝ • **FINISHED QUILT:** 70˝ × 72½˝

Do those delicious fat quarter bundles of rainbow-colored fabrics make you drool? This project is perfect for using a bundle of beautiful fabric or pulling a whole range of colors from your stash.

For this quilt, I used fabrics from a fat quarter pack of Jasmine by Valori Wells for Robert Kaufman Fabrics and combined them with two grays for the background. I love Valori's lino-print effects, and the cute camels were irresistible! My camels are walking in their caravan amid the desert sunset.

MATERIALS

3 orange prints: 1 fat quarter of each

3 violet prints: 1 fat quarter of each

3 blue prints: 1 fat quarter of each

3 turquoise prints:
1 fat quarter of each

3 yellow/green prints:
1 fat quarter of each

Medium gray: 1⅛ yards

Dark gray: 2⅛ yards

Assorted black-and-white prints:
8 fat quarters

Binding: ⅝ yard

Backing: 4½ yards

Batting: 78˝ × 80˝

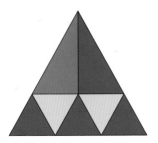

The large half-triangles of the two grays give the quilt an almost 3D effect, and the variety of black-and-white prints in the small triangles gives a little extra sparkle. I included prints from almost solid white to tone-on-tone black, including gray and high-contrast black and white.

🔴 TIP Building a Rainbow Effect

A rainbow quilt can include a different set of colors depending on the hues you love. Play with different places on the color wheel and focus on the colors that appeal to you most. *Caravan* uses five different hues.

Blue, violet, magenta, lime, and turquoise are mostly cool hues.

Take out the turquoise and magenta; then add in orange and yellow for a lighter look.

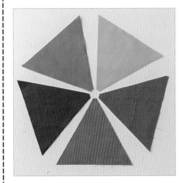

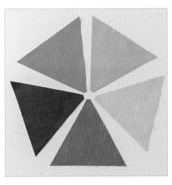

A rich effect is achieved by removing the yellow.

Next time you are in your local quilt shop, notice how fabric designers play with the spectrum when they curate the colors in their ranges. One rainbow is never the same as another!

CUTTING

*For more detailed cutting instructions, see
60° Triangle Basics (page 29). Remember,
if you are using a straight ruler to cut the
triangles, start with a strip ¼″ wider than
the size listed. You may need more strips for
cutting directional fabrics or fussy cutting.
When cutting half-width-of-fabric strips
from fat quarters, cut perpendicular to the
selvage for strips approximately 22″ long.*

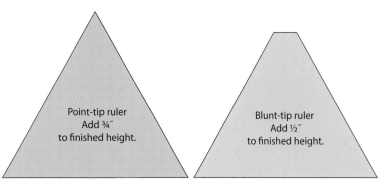

Point-tip ruler
Add ¾″
to finished height.

Blunt-tip ruler
Add ½″
to finished height.

SHAPE	CUT SIZE	FIRST, CUT FABRIC STRIPS:	SUBCUT FROM STRIPS:
5 color groups: Cut from *each* fat quarter:			
8″ triangle	8½″ tall, 10⅛″ base	1 strip (3 total) 8½″* × half width of fabric	2 triangles (6 total)
4″ triangle	4½″ tall, 5½″ base	1 strip (3 total) 4½″* × half width of fabric	6 triangles (18 total)
Medium gray			
8″ half-triangle	9³⁄₁₆″ × 5⁵⁄₁₆″	3 strips 9³⁄₁₆″ × width of fabric	30 half-triangles from 15 rectangles 9³⁄₁₆″ × 5⁵⁄₁₆″. *Cut the rectangles in half diagonally in just one direction: from top right to bottom left.*
Dark gray			
8″ half-triangle	9³⁄₁₆″ × 5⁵⁄₁₆″	3 strips 9³⁄₁₆″ × width of fabric	30 half-triangles from 15 rectangles 9³⁄₁₆″ × 5⁵⁄₁₆″. *Cut the rectangles in half diagonally in just one direction: from top left to bottom right.*
4″ triangle	4½″ tall, 5½″ base	7 strips 4½″* × width of fabric	84 triangles
4″ half-triangle	5³⁄₁₆″ × 3″	1 strip 5³⁄₁₆″ × width of fabric	12 half-triangles from 6 rectangles 5³⁄₁₆″ × 3″. Cut half the rectangles diagonally in one direction and half in the opposite.
Assorted black-and-white prints: Cut from *each* fat quarter:			
4″ triangle	4½″ tall, 5½″ base	3 strips 4½″* × half width of fabric (24 strips total)	15 triangles (120 total)
Binding			
8 strips 2½″ × width of fabric			

*If using a straight ruler to cut the triangles, start with a strip ¼″ wider than the size listed. The cut size of your triangle will be ¼″ taller than the cut size in the chart.

Construction

Seam allowances are ¼˝ unless otherwise noted. Press all seams open.

Make the Blocks

Follow the step-by-step instructions for making the Simply Triangles block (page 39).

1. In each of the 5 color groupings, make 2 blocks in each of 3 fabric combinations.

Use 2 fabrics from the same color group for each block—1 fabric for the large triangle and a second fabric for 3 small triangles, rotating the fabrics. Distribute the small black-and-white triangles among the blocks to give a pleasing effect over the whole quilt. **FIGS. A–C**

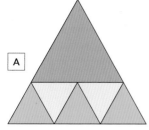

Block using fabrics 1 and 2:
Make 2 in each color group.

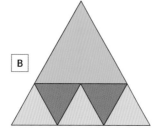

Block using fabrics 2 and 3:
Make 2 in each color group.

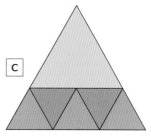

Block using fabrics 3 and 1:
Make 2 in each color group.

---

2. Join pairs of medium gray and dark gray half-triangles to make 8˝ triangles. These will be the large triangles in the gray Simply Triangles blocks. Complete the block with 3 small dark gray triangles and 2 small black-and-white print triangles. Make 24. **FIG. D**

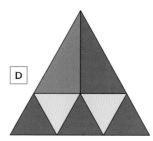

Make 24.

3. Join a small dark gray triangle, a small black-and-white print triangle, and a small dark gray half-triangle in a row, as shown. Add a large dark gray half-triangle to the top to complete a half block. Make 6. **FIG. E**

4. Join a small dark gray triangle, a small black-and-white print triangle, and a small dark gray half-triangle in a row, as shown. Add a large medium-gray half-triangle to the top to complete a half block. Make 6. **FIG. F**

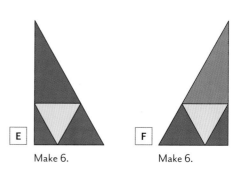

Make 6.   Make 6.

Quilt Assembly

1. Referring to the quilt assembly diagram, arrange the blocks in 6 rows. Use the half blocks to fill in the right and left sides of the quilt.

2. Sew the blocks together in rows. Sew the rows together.

Quilt assembly

TIP **Use a Design Wall**

For a quilt like this, which is quite scrappy, a design wall is invaluable. The placement of the light and dark black-and-white prints makes a big difference to the look, and it is good to balance these out across the quilt. You can also play with the positions of the various colored blocks until you are happy with the look.

My 8′ × 8′ design wall is made of a flannel backing fabric stretched over bulletin board and stapled to the back. You can install it permanently on the wall or make a smaller more portable wall. If you cannot find a flannel backing fabric, use a flannel sheet or buy a gridded gray design-wall fabric.

Finishing the Quilt

Quilt and bind the quilt as desired. I used dark gray for the binding to keep the focus on the pattern in the quilt.

For this quilt, Sue used a decorative pattern inside each of the large triangles and combined it with a simple straight-line pattern in the small triangles. Treating the large and small shapes separately emphasizes the design.

Detail of *Caravan*

Caravan, 70˝ × 72½˝, designed and pieced by Sheila Christensen, quilted by Sue Burnett

SKILL LEVEL: Beginner

After the Storm

FINISHED BLOCK HEIGHT: 12˝ · **FINISHED QUILT:** 70˝ × 72½˝

After the storm comes a rainbow. The fun in this quilt is the joy of playing with bright colors until you have just the combination you love.

I arranged my blocks so that the intense yellow triangle would make it seem like a bolt of lightning was striking through the quilt. My quilt has very intense rainbow colors, but you don't have to stick exactly to the hues I picked. Emphasize your favorite colors and leave out ones you are not so keen on. Saturated hues work best, as you really need them to shine.

MATERIALS

Feature prints: ⅜ yard *each* of 6 colors—yellow, orange, red/magenta, violet, blue, and turquoise

Blender prints: ¼ yard *each* of the following:

  1 light and 1 medium chartreuse

  1 light and 1 medium orange

  1 light and 1 medium magenta

  1 light and 1 medium violet

  1 light and 1 medium blue

  1 light and 1 medium turquoise

Dark gray: 2⅝ yards

Medium gray: ⅝ yard

Light gray: ½ yard

Spotted gray: ½ yard

Binding: ⅝ yard

Backing: 4½ yards

Batting: 78˝ × 80˝

CUTTING

For step-by-step cutting instructions, see 60° Triangle Basics (page 29). Remember, if you are using a straight ruler to cut the triangles, start with a strip ¼˝ wider than the size listed. You may need more strips for cutting directional fabrics or fussy cutting.

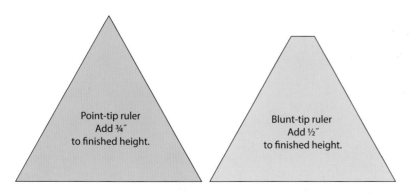

Point-tip ruler
Add ¾˝
to finished height.

Blunt-tip ruler
Add ½˝
to finished height.

SHAPE	CUT SIZE	FIRST, CUT FABRIC STRIPS:	SUBCUT FROM STRIPS:
6 assorted feature prints: Cut from *each* print:			
8″ triangle	8½″ tall, 10⅛″ base	1 strip (6 total) 8½″* × width of fabric	3 triangles (18 total)
Assorted blender prints: Cut from *each* light chartreuse, medium orange, medium magenta, medium violet, light blue, and medium turquoise:			
4″ triangle	4½″ tall, 5½″ base	1 strip 4½″* × width of fabric	6 triangles (36 total)
Assorted blender prints: Cut from *each* medium chartreuse, light orange, light magenta, light violet, medium blue, and light turquoise:			
4″ triangle	4½″ tall, 5½″ base	1 strip 4½″* × width of fabric	9 triangles (54 total)
Dark gray			
8″ triangle	8½″ tall, 10⅛″ base	4 strips 8½″* × width of fabric	24 triangles
12″ half-triangle	13³⁄₁₆″ × 7⅝″	4 strips 13³⁄₁₆″ × width of fabric	From each strip, cut 1 rectangle 13³⁄₁₆″ × 7⅝″ (4 total). Cut 8 half-triangles from these 4 rectangles. Cut half the rectangles in one direction and half in the opposite.
Angled-end rectangles	12½″ × 28½″		Trim the remainder of each strip to 12½″ wide. Cut 4 rectangles 12½″ × 28½″. Cut one end of each rectangle at 60°, with 2 angled in one direction and 2 in the opposite direction, as shown.
Medium gray			
4″ triangle	4½″ tall, 5½″ base	4 strips 4½″* × width of fabric	48 triangles
Light gray			
4″ triangle	4½″ tall, 5½″ base	3 strips 4½″* × width of fabric	36 triangles
Spotted gray			
4″ triangle	4½″ tall, 5½″ base	3 strips 4½″* × width of fabric	36 triangles
Binding			
8 strips 2½″ × width of fabric			

If using a straight ruler to cut the triangles, start with a strip ¼″ wider than the size listed. The cut size of your triangle will be ¼″ taller than the cut size in the chart.

Construction

Seam allowances are ¼˝ unless otherwise noted. Press all seams open.

Make the Blocks

Follow the step-by-step instructions for making the Simply Triangles block (page 39).

1. Make 3 blocks in *each* of the 6 color combinations:

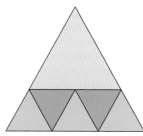

Yellow/chartreuse: Make 3.

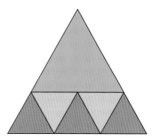

Orange: Make 3.

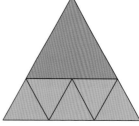

Magenta: Make 3.

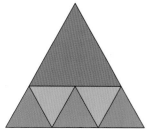

Violet: Make 3.

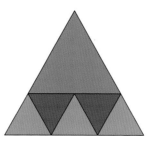

Blue: Make 3.

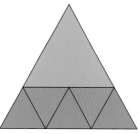

Turquoise: Make 3.

---

2. Use 1 large dark gray triangle, 2 small medium-gray triangles, and 3 small light gray triangles to make a block. Make 12.

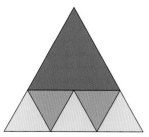

Make 12.

3. Use 1 large dark gray triangle, 2 small medium-gray triangles, and 3 small spotted triangles to make a block. Make 12.

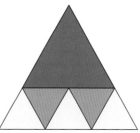

Make 12.

Quilt Assembly

1. Referring to the quilt assembly diagram, arrange the blocks in rows with the background rectangles and half-triangles.

2. Sew the blocks, triangles, and rectangles together in rows. Sew the rows together.

Finishing the Quilt

The quilting can be kept very simple, just as for *Caravan*. Sue quilted a decorative swirl inside the large triangles and filled the small triangles with a simple line pattern.

Quilt assembly

Detail of *After the Storm*

After the Storm, 70˝ × 72½˝, designed and pieced by Sheila Christensen, quilted by Sue Burnett

LESSON TWO:
60° TRAPEZOID

60° TRAPEZOID BASICS

Half a Hexie?

A trapezoid is a triangle with the top part cut off.

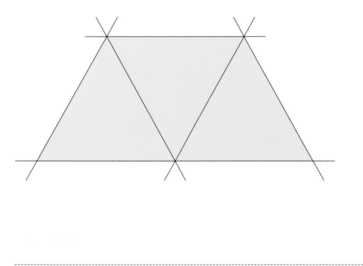

Two trapezoids together can make a hexagon shape.

Longer trapezoids make a lozenge shape when joined.

How Trapezoid Sizes Are Defined

All trapezoids can be measured by their height × the length of the base—the longest horizontal line. In the cutting charts, you will find this size listed in the Cut Size column.

If the trapezoid can be cut with a triangle ruler, I have labelled it with two numbers with an × between and no inch marks: 2 × 4, for example. These two measurements are based on the grid size.

The first number determines the width of strip that you need to cut, and the second tells you where to place the triangle ruler.

For example, a 2 × 4 trapezoid is 2 grid units high and 4 grid units wide at the base. It will be 2˝ high when finished and will be the equivalent width of a 4˝ (finished-size) triangle. If you cut trapezoids with a triangle ruler, all you need to know is that the 2 indicates the strip width that you need (add ½˝ for seams to make the strip 2½˝), and the 4 indicates the ruler line you need to use for cutting (add ¾˝ for point-tip rulers or ½˝ for blunt-tip rulers).

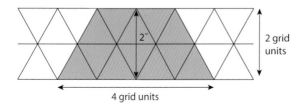

A 2 × 6 trapezoid is 2 grid units high and 6 grid units wide at the base, the equivalent width of a 6˝ triangle. Cut a 2½˝ strip and use the 6¾˝ (point-tip ruler) or 6½˝ ruler line (blunt-tip ruler).

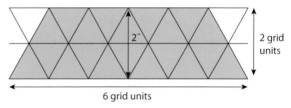

If the trapezoid is too large to be cut with a triangle ruler, I have labelled it as an oversize trapezoid in the Shape column of the cutting charts. Refer to the Cut Size column to see the strip width and base length.

Cutting 60° Trapezoids

Using a Triangle Ruler

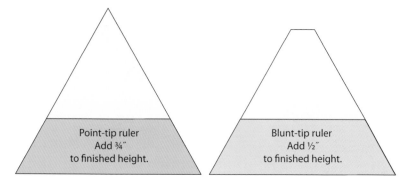

Point-tip ruler
Add ¾˝
to finished height.

Blunt-tip ruler
Add ½˝
to finished height.

1. Start by cutting a strip of fabric ½˝ wider than the finished height of the trapezoid. For a 2 × 4 trapezoid, cut a strip 2½˝ × width of fabric. See Cutting Strips (page 23).

2. Place the triangle ruler on the strip and cut both sides.

- **If you are using a point-tip ruler,** add ¾˝ to the width of the shape. To cut a 2 × 4 trapezoid, place the 4¾˝ line on the bottom of the strip. **FIG. A**

- **If you are using a blunt-tip ruler,** add ½˝ to the width of the shape. Place the 4½˝ line on the bottom of the strip. Cut on the right and left sides of the ruler. **FIG. B**

3. Continue cutting more trapezoids by rotating the ruler and cutting again. **FIG. C**

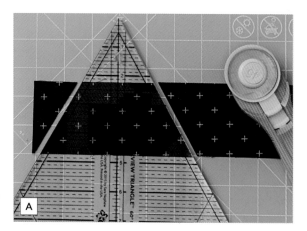

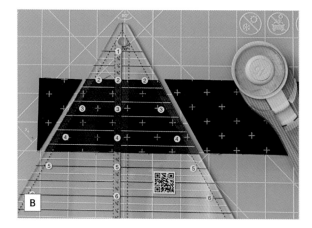

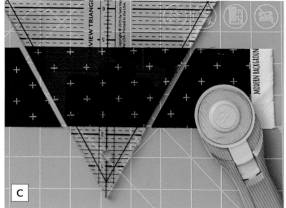

Using a Straight Ruler

If you do not have a triangle ruler or your ruler is smaller than the ruler line shown in the chart (next page), follow this method for cutting trapezoids.

1. Start with a strip the width shown in the chart. For example, for a 3 × 9 trapezoid, start with a 3½˝ strip. Cut a 60° angle on the left end of the strip. **FIG. A**

2. Measure the trapezoid base along the top of the strip and make a mark. For a 3 × 9 trapezoid, the base is 11⅝⁄₁₆˝. **FIG. B**

3. Cut another 60° angle at the mark, this time in the opposite direction of the first angle. **FIG. C**

4. To cut more trapezoids from the same strip, measure along the bottom of the strip for the next trapezoid. Cut a 60° angle.

Cutting Trapezoids from Rectangles

You also can cut a trapezoid by first cutting a rectangle equal to the unfinished height and base of the trapezoid. This information is in the Cut Size column of the cutting charts. Cut each end of the rectangle at a 60° angle in opposite directions. A caveat, though: I reserve this method for cutting just a few trapezoids at a time, because it wastes the small half-triangles you cut off the ends. If the cutting chart tells you to cut multiple trapezoids from a strip, you will need more fabric to use this method instead. Be sure you have enough fabric to cut one or more extra strips.

TIP **Using the Optional Patterns**

If you are not sure how to line up your ruler, you can use a pattern (pages 60 and 61) for the smaller sizes to check the size.

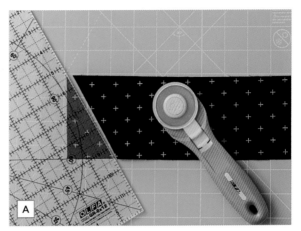

Cutting a 60° angle with a straight ruler

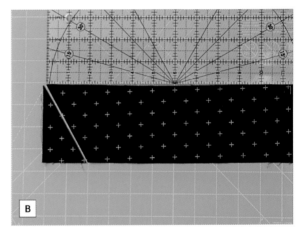

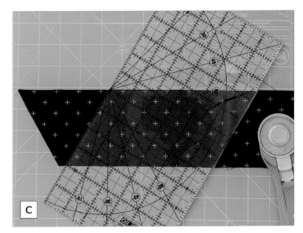

Using a straight ruler

Quick Reference: Cutting 60° Trapezoids

This chart includes all the standard trapezoid sizes you could cut with a triangle ruler. The exact base measurements (used for straight-ruler cutting) would fall at odd places along the inch marker; I've rounded them to the closest 1/16″. You can round up to the nearest 1/8″ if necessary, but your cutting will not be as accurate.

TRAPEZOID SIZE	STRIP WIDTH	POINT-TIP RULER LINE	BLUNT-TIP RULER LINE	STRAIGHT RULER: LENGTH OF TRAPEZOID BASE
1 × 2		2¾″	2½″	3³⁄₁₆″
1 × 3		3¾″	3½″	4⅜″
1 × 4	1½″	4¾″	4½″	5½″
1 × 5		5¾″	5½″	6¹¹⁄₁₆″
1 × 6		6¾″	6½″	7¹³⁄₁₆″
2 × 3		3¾″	3½″	4⅜″
2 × 4		4¾″	4½″	5½″
2 × 5		5¾″	5½″	6¹¹⁄₁₆″
2 × 6		6¾″	6½″	7¹³⁄₁₆″
2 × 7		7¾″	7½″	9″
2 × 8	2½″	8¾″	8½″	10⅛″
2 × 9		9¾″	9½″	11⁵⁄₁₆″
2 × 10		10¾″	10½″	12⁷⁄₁₆″
2 × 11		11¾″	11½″	13⅝″
2 × 12		(none)	12½	14¾″
3 × 4		4¾″	4½″	5½″
3 × 5		5¾″	5½″	6¹¹⁄₁₆″
3 × 6		6¾″	6½″	7¹³⁄₁₆″
3 × 7		7¾″	7½″	9″
3 × 8	3½″	8¾″	8½″	10⅛″
3 × 9		9¾″	9½″	11⁵⁄₁₆″
3 × 10		10¾″	10½″	12⁷⁄₁₆″
3 × 11		11¾″	11½″	13⅝″
3 × 12		(none)	12½″	14¾″

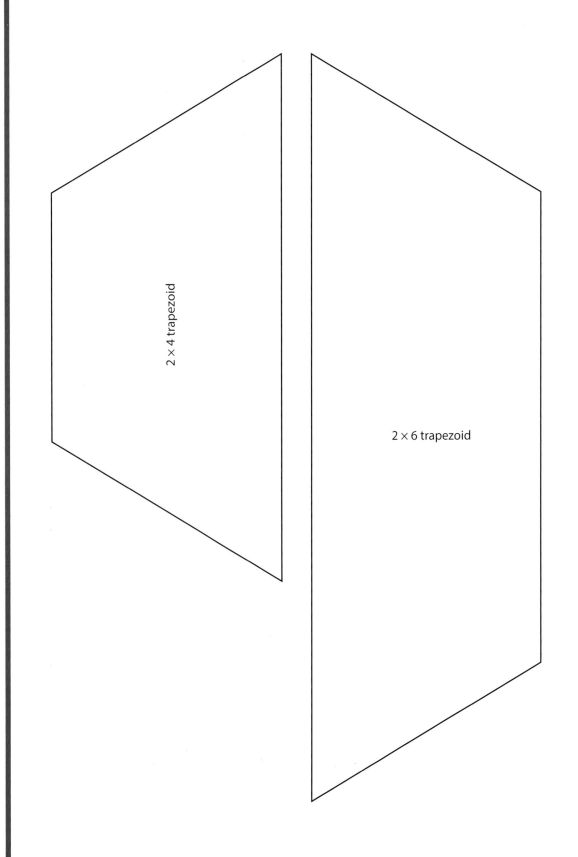

2 × 4 trapezoid

2 × 6 trapezoid

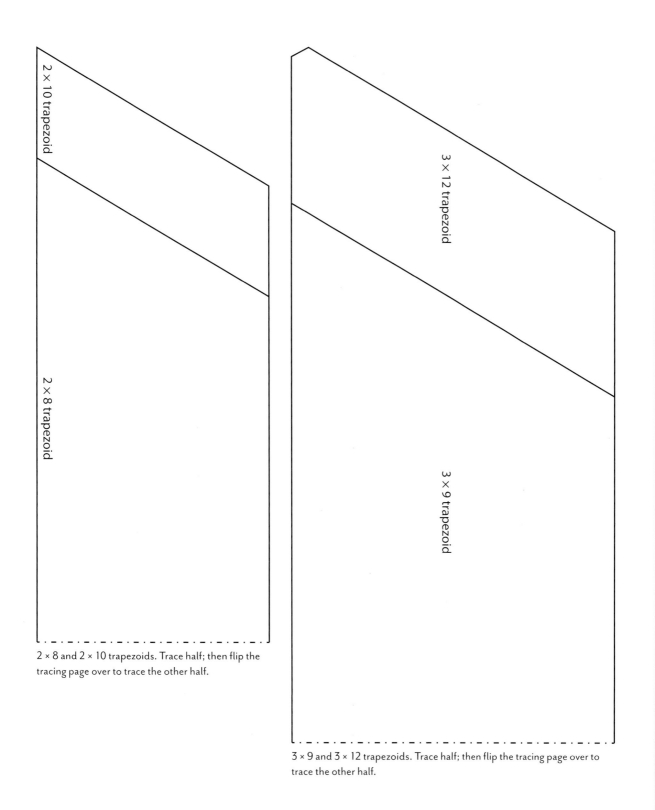

2 × 10 trapezoid

2 × 8 trapezoid

3 × 12 trapezoid

3 × 9 trapezoid

2 × 8 and 2 × 10 trapezoids. Trace half; then flip the tracing page over to trace the other half.

3 × 9 and 3 × 12 trapezoids. Trace half; then flip the tracing page over to trace the other half.

Peak Block

FINISHED BLOCK HEIGHT: 12˝

This block is so simple and yet so versatile.

Two possible ways of combining the block are shown in *Mirror Mirror* and *Court and Spark*.

MATERIALS

Black: 1 strip 3½˝ × width of fabric

White: 1 strip 6½˝ × half width of fabric

CUTTING

For step-by-step cutting instructions, see *60° Triangle Basics (page 29)* and *60° Trapezoid Basics (page 55)*. Remember, if you are using a straight ruler to cut the triangles, start with a strip ¼˝ wider than the size listed. You may need more strips for cutting directional fabrics or fussy cutting.

SHAPE	CUT SIZE	FIRST, CUT FABRIC STRIPS:	SUBCUT FROM STRIPS:
Black			
3 × 9 trapezoid	3½˝ tall, 11⁵⁄₁₆˝ base	1 strip 3½˝ × width of fabric	1 trapezoid
3 × 12 trapezoid	3½˝ tall, 14¾˝ base		1 trapezoid
White			
6˝ triangle	6½˝ tall, 7¹³⁄₁₆˝ base	1 strip 6½˝* × half width of fabric	1 triangle

If using a straight ruler to cut the triangles, start with a strip ¼˝ wider than the size listed. The cut size of your triangle will be ¼˝ taller than the cut size in the chart.

Make the Block

Seam allowances are ¼˝ unless otherwise noted. Press all seams open.

1. Line up the white triangle with the 3 × 9 black trapezoid on the right. **FIG. A**

2. Place the trapezoid right sides together with the triangle. Sew. Press the seam open. **FIG. B**

3. Line up the 3 × 12 black trapezoid on the left. **FIG. C**

4. Sew. Press the seams open. **FIGS. D & E**

A

B

C

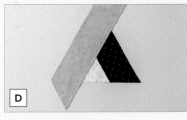
D

E

Peak block

Quilting suggestion for Peak block

Mirror Mirror

FINISHED BLOCK HEIGHT: 12˝ · **FINISHED QUILT:** 70˝ × 84½˝

The fabrics I used in this quilt are from Modern Backgrounds Luster by Brigitte Heitland of Zen Chic for Moda. These neutral fabrics are plain enough to really show the piecing, yet they have interest when you look up close at the detail.

The key to this bold, dramatic design is to have a high level of contrast between the dark and light fabrics.

MATERIALS

White: ¼ yard

Black: 2¼ yards

Gold: ⅞ yard

Black with gold: 1⅝ yards

Gray: 1¾ yards

Binding: ¾ yard

Backing: 5⅛ yards

Batting: 78˝ × 92˝

CUTTING

For step-by-step cutting instructions, see 60° Triangle Basics (page 29) and 60° Trapezoid Basics (page 55). Remember, if you are using a straight ruler to cut the triangles, start with a strip ¼˝ wider than the size listed. You may need more strips for cutting directional fabrics or fussy cutting.

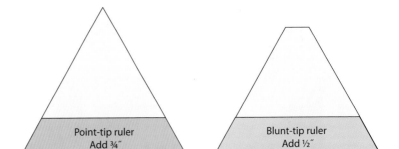

| Point-tip ruler Add ¾˝ to finished height. | Blunt-tip ruler Add ½˝ to finished height. |

SHAPE	CUT SIZE	FOR	FIRST, CUT FABRIC STRIPS:	SUBCUT FROM STRIPS:
White				
△ 6˝ triangle	6½˝ tall, 7¹³⁄₁₆˝ base	Block A	1 strip 6½˝* × width of fabric	5 triangles
Black				
3 × 9 trapezoid	3½˝ tall, 11⁵⁄₁₆˝ base	Blocks A and B	9 strips 3½˝ × width of fabric	35 trapezoids
3 × 12 trapezoid	3½˝ tall, 14¾˝ base	Blocks A and B	12 strips 3½˝ × width of fabric	35 trapezoids
Gold				
△ 6˝ triangle	6½˝ tall, 7¹³⁄₁₆˝ base	Block B	4 strips 6½˝* × width of fabric	30 triangles

SHAPE	CUT SIZE	FOR	FIRST, CUT FABRIC STRIPS:	SUBCUT FROM STRIPS:
Black with gold				
6˝ triangle	6½˝ tall, 7¹³⁄₁₆˝ base	Block C	4 strips 6½˝* × width of fabric	28 triangles
12˝ half-triangles	13³⁄₁₆˝ × 7⅝˝	Setting triangles	2 strips 13³⁄₁₆˝ × width of fabric	16 half-triangles from 8 rectangles 13³⁄₁₆˝ × 7⅝˝. Cut half the rectangles in one direction and half in the opposite. There will be 2 extra triangles.
Gray				
3 × 9 trapezoid	3½˝ tall, 11⁵⁄₁₆˝ base	Block C	7 strips 3½˝ × width of fabric	28 trapezoids
3 × 12 trapezoid	3½˝ tall, 14¾˝ base	Block C	10 strips 3½˝ × width of fabric	28 trapezoids
Binding				
			9 strips 2½˝ × width of fabric	

If using a straight ruler to cut the triangles, start with a strip ¼˝ wider than the size listed. The cut size of your triangle will be ¼˝ taller than the cut size in the chart.

Construction

Seam allowances are ¼˝ unless otherwise noted. Press all seams open.

Make the Blocks

Follow the step-by-step instructions for making the Peak block (page 62).

1. Make 5 Blocks A using a white triangle and black trapezoids. **FIG. A**

2. Make 30 Blocks B using a gold triangle and black trapezoids. **FIG. B**

3. Make 28 Blocks C using a black-with-gold triangle and gray trapezoids. **FIG. C**

Detail of *Mirror Mirror*

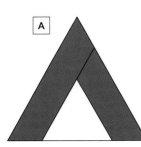

Block A: Make 5.

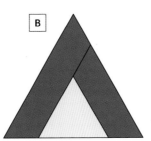

Block B: Make 30.

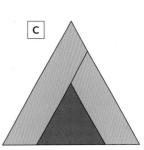

Block C: Make 28.

Quilt Assembly

1. Referring to the quilt assembly diagram, arrange the blocks and side half-triangles in rows.

2. Sew the triangles and blocks together in rows; then sew the rows together.

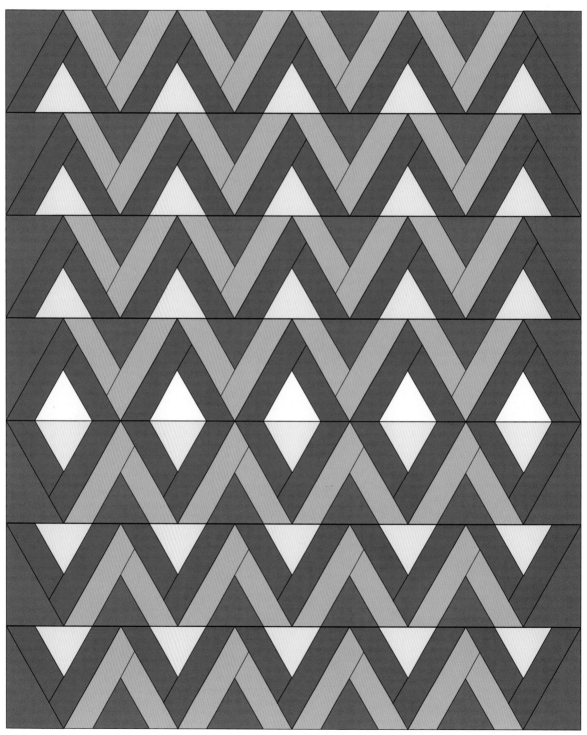

Quilt assembly

Finishing the Quilt

Quilt and bind the quilt as desired. *Mirror Mirror* was quilted by Sue Burnett on a longarm machine using patterns designed specifically for 60° blocks by Sharon Perry of House of Creations.

See another idea for quilting the Peak block (page 62). An alternative would be to quilt lines ¼˝–½˝ from the seams and then free-motion quilt inside the blocks. Big-stitch hand quilting would look really effective and would add some texture to this bold look.

Mirror Mirror, 70˝ × 84½˝, designed and pieced by Sheila Christensen, quilted by Sue Burnett

Court and Spark

FINISHED BLOCK HEIGHT: 12˝ · **FINISHED QUILT:** 56˝ × 60½˝

Do you see a star or a hexagon? The optical illusions in this design stand out the most when you use highly contrasting colors. These Modern Backgrounds Luster fabrics by Brigitte Heitland of Zen Chic for Moda are very subtly overprinted in metallic gold, giving the quilt a neutral palette with a sophisticated touch. If you have a minimalist decor, this would be the perfect accent—either as a centerpiece on a bed or as a wall decoration.

MATERIALS

Black with gold: ½ yard

White: ⅞ yard

Black: ⅞ yard

Light gold: ½ yard

Gold: 1½ yards for background

Binding: ½ yard

Backing: 3⅝ yards

Batting: 64˝ × 68˝

CUTTING

For step-by-step cutting instructions, see 60° Triangle Basics (page 29) and 60° Trapezoid Basics (page 55). Remember, if you are using a straight ruler to cut the triangles, start with a strip ¼˝ wider than the size listed. You may need more strips for cutting directional fabrics or fussy cutting.

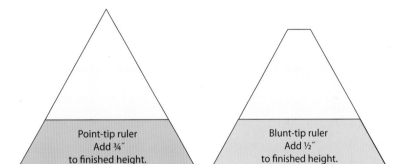

Point-tip ruler
Add ¾˝
to finished height.

Blunt-tip ruler
Add ½˝
to finished height.

SHAPE	CUT SIZE	FOR	FIRST, CUT FABRIC STRIPS:	SUBCUT FROM STRIPS:
Black with gold				
6˝ triangle	6½˝ tall, 7¹³⁄₁₆˝ base	Block A	2 strips 6½˝* × width of fabric	12 triangles
White				
3 × 9 trapezoid	3½˝ tall, 11⁵⁄₁₆˝ base	Block A	3 strips 3½˝ × width of fabric	12 trapezoids
3 × 12 trapezoid	3½˝ tall, 14¾˝ base	Block A	4 strips 3½˝ × width of fabric	12 trapezoids
Black				
3 × 9 trapezoid	3½˝ tall, 11⁵⁄₁₆˝ base	Block B	3 strips 3½˝ × width of fabric	12 trapezoids
3 × 12 trapezoid	3½˝ tall, 14¾˝ base	Block B	4 strips 3½˝ × width of fabric	12 trapezoids

SHAPE	CUT SIZE	FOR	FIRST, CUT FABRIC STRIPS:	SUBCUT FROM STRIPS:
Light gold				
6˝ triangle	6½˝ tall, 7¹³⁄₁₆˝ base	Block B	2 strips 6½˝* × width of fabric	12 triangles
Gold				
12˝ half-triangles	13³⁄₁₆˝ × 7⅝˝	Setting	2 strips 13³⁄₁₆˝ × width of fabric	Cut 1 rectangle 13³⁄₁₆˝ × 7⅝˝ from each strip. Cut each rectangle in half in opposite directions.
Angled-end rectangles	12½˝ tall, 14¾˝ base			Trim the remainder of each strip to 12½˝ wide. Cut 4 rectangles 12½˝ × 14¾˝. Cut one end of each rectangle at 60°, with 2 angled in one direction and 2 in the opposite direction.
Borders	6½˝ wide	Borders	3 strips 6½˝ × width of fabric	Subcut 1 border strip in half. Sew each whole strip to a half strip. Trim the borders to 56˝ long for the top and bottom borders.
Binding				
6 strips 2½˝ × width of fabric				

If using a straight ruler to cut the triangles, start with a strip ¼˝ wider than the size listed. The cut size of your triangle will be ¼˝ taller than the cut size in the chart.

Construction

Seam allowances are ¼˝ unless otherwise noted. Press all seams open.

Make the Blocks

Follow the step-by-step instructions for making the Peak block (page 62).

1. Make 12 Blocks A using a black-with-gold triangle and white trapezoids. **FIG. A**

2. Make 12 Blocks B using a light gold triangle and black trapezoids. **FIG. B**

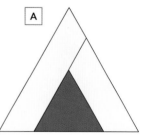

Block A: Make 12.

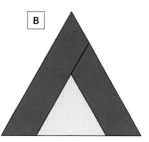

Block B: Make 12.

Quilt Assembly

1. Referring to the quilt assembly diagram, arrange the blocks, rectangles, and background triangles.

2. Sew the triangles, rectangles, and blocks together in rows; then sew the rows together.

3. Attach a border strip to the top and bottom of the quilt.

Quilt assembly

Finishing the Quilt

Quilt and bind the quilt as desired. *Court and Spark* was quilted on a longarm machine using patterns designed specifically for 60° blocks. Alternatively, quilt ¼˝–½˝ away from the seams and then add free-motion or straight-line quilting inside the blocks. The background area would be a great negative space for getting creative with your free-motion quilting.

Court and Spark, 56˝ × 60½˝, designed and pieced by Sheila Christensen, quilted by Sue Burnett

LESSON THREE: 60° DIAMOND

60° DIAMOND BASICS

A Girl's Best Friend

A diamond is made up of two triangles.

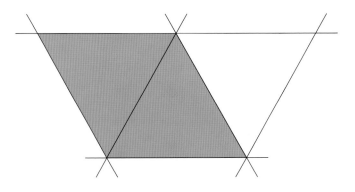

How Diamond Sizes Are Defined

Diamond sizes are labelled by the finished distance between parallel sides. This makes it easy to cut and fit them in with the other 60° shapes.

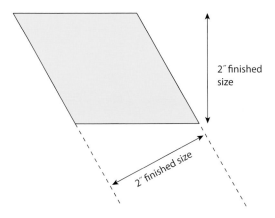

A 2″ finished-size diamond is 2″ across from flat side to flat side, and the finished height from point to point is 4″. It is 4 grid units high from point to point and 2 grid units wide from point to point.

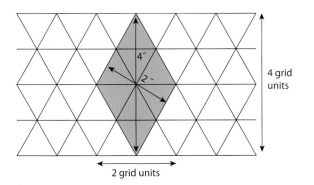

Cutting 60° Diamonds

There are two methods for cutting 60° diamonds.

If your fabric print doesn't have a directional pattern, use the first method shown below, which uses fabric economically. With directional prints like a stripe, however, using this method will put the pattern on an angle in the block.

If you wish to keep the pattern vertical, see Cutting Upright Diamonds from Directional Fabric (page 76).

Cutting Diamonds from Nondirectional Fabric

1. For a 2″ finished-size diamond, start with a 2½″ strip. Make a 60° cut on one end.

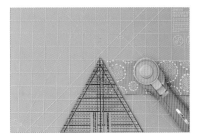

Using a triangle ruler

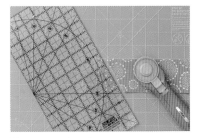

Using a straight ruler

2. Use a straight ruler to measure 2½˝ across from the angled cut and make a second cut.

You can continue to cut more diamonds along the fabric strip using the straight ruler. FIGS. A & B

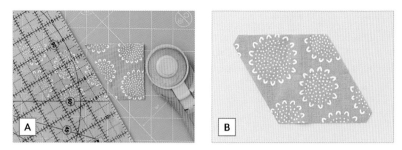

The straight grain will align with 2 sides of the diamond instead of running vertically from top to bottom. This is acceptable when constructing the Stack the Dishes block, and it can create some interesting patterns when the blocks are combined.

Cutting Upright Diamonds from Directional Fabric

These methods work for directional fabrics and are the basis for fussy cutting pieces.

USING A TRIANGLE RULER

1. For a 2˝ finished-size diamond, start with a 4½˝ strip. Fold the strip in half lengthwise and place the triangle ruler on the strip. FIGS. C & D

2. Cut on both sides and open out. FIG. E

USING A STRAIGHT RULER

Start with a rectangle the size shown in the chart (page 78).

1. For a 2˝ finished diamond, cut a strip 4½˝ wide. Subcut a rectangle 4½˝ × 2⅞˝. FIG. F

2. Fold the rectangle in half across the long sides. With the fold at the bottom, place the 60° angle of the ruler on the fold and cut. FIG. G

3. Rotate the fabric, turn the ruler in the other direction, and cut again. FIG. H

4. Open the diamond. It will have blunt tips and measure 2½˝ from straight edge to straight edge.

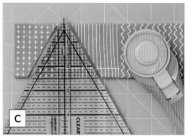

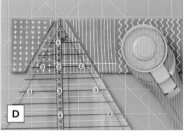

Point-tip ruler: Place the 2½˝ line on the fold.

Blunt-tip ruler: Place the 2¼˝ line on the fold.

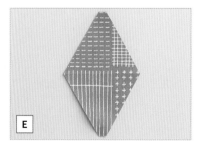

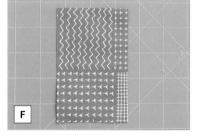

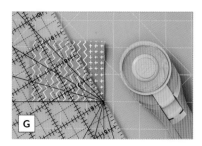

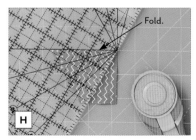

FUSSY CUTTING 60° DIAMONDS

If you have a fabric with a feature that you want to highlight, you can fussy cut diamonds to make the most of the design.

The following instructions are for a 2˝ finished diamond, which will be 4˝ finished from tip to tip.

1. Start by cutting a 4½˝ strip, with the design you want centered along the strip. Here I have used ruler tape to mark where the seams will be at the top and bottom of the diamond. **FIG. A**

2. Fold the strip lengthwise with the fold at the bottom. **FIG. B**

3. Place the triangle ruler with the line on the fold and the tip at the cut edges. For a point-tip ruler, use the 4½˝ line; for a blunt-tip ruler, use the 4¼˝ line. **FIG. C**

4. Cut on both sides of the ruler. **FIG. D**

5. Open out. **FIG. E**

To cut more identical pieces, place a cut diamond on the strip and align the pattern. Use this to guide the ruler placement for the next cut. **FIG. F**

If you are using a straight ruler, start with the 4½˝ strip as directed above; then follow the directions for cutting diamonds from directional fabric (previous page), centering your motif when you subcut the 4½˝ × 2⅞˝ rectangle (or whatever the correct size is for your project).

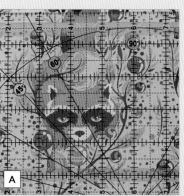

A

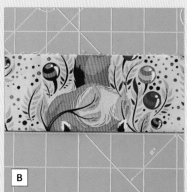

B

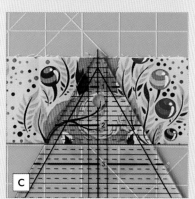

C

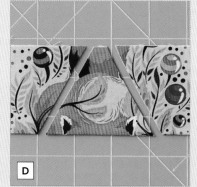

D

E

F

Quick Reference: Cutting 60° Diamonds

CUTTING UPRIGHT DIAMONDS FROM DIRECTIONAL FABRIC

FINISHED SIZE	STRIP WIDTH	POINT-TIP TRIANGLE RULER LINE	BLUNT-TIP TRIANGLE RULER LINE	STRAIGHT RULER Along the fold, measure the approximate width of the diamond from point to point.
		Fold strip in half and place ruler on fold.		*Fold strip in half.*
1″	2½″	1½″	1¼″	1¾″
2″	4½″	2½″	2¼″	2⅞″
3″	6½″	3½″	3¼″	4¹⁄₁₆″
4″	8½″	4½″	4¼″	5³⁄₁₆″
5″	10½″	5½″	5¼″	6⅜″
6″	12½″	6½″	6¼″	7½″
7″	14½″	7½″	7¼″	8¹¹⁄₁₆″
8″	16½″	8½″	8¼″	9¹³⁄₁₆″
9″	18½″	9½″	9¼″	11″
10″	20½″	10½″	10¼″	12⅛″

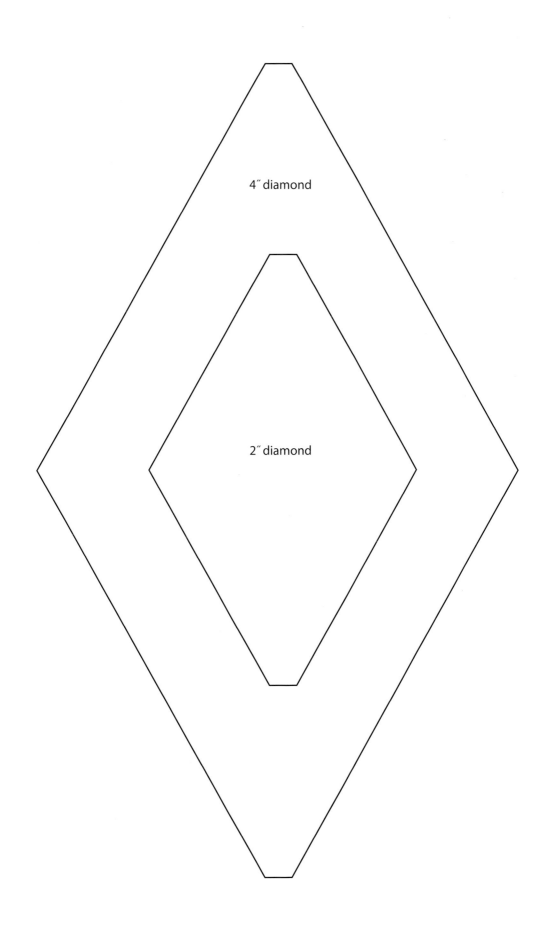

4″ diamond

2″ diamond

Stack the Dishes Block

FINISHED BLOCK HEIGHT: 12˝

Whether in a straight setting such as *Misty Morning* or a kaleidoscope setting like *Shadowflower*, the Stack the Dishes block creates a beautiful effect when repeated.

Detail of *Shadowflower* (page 87). See how the diamonds in the Stack the Dishes block combine to form a star when the blocks are set pointing inward.

MATERIALS

Feature: 1 strip 2½˝ × width of fabric, plus 1 square 4½˝ × 4½˝ for the diamond if you are using directional fabric

Background (white): 1 strip 2½˝ × width of fabric

CUTTING

For step-by-step cutting instructions, see 60° Triangle Basics (page 29), 60° Trapezoid Basics (page 55), and 60° Diamond Basics (page 74). Remember, if you are using a straight ruler to cut the triangles, start with a strip ¼˝ wider than the size listed. You may need more strips for cutting directional fabrics or fussy cutting.

SHAPE	CUT SIZE	FIRST, CUT FABRIC STRIPS:	SUBCUT FROM STRIPS:
Feature fabric			
2˝ triangle	2½˝ tall, 3³⁄₁₆˝ base	1 strip 2½˝* × width of fabric	4 triangles
2 × 6 trapezoid	2½˝ tall, 7¹³⁄₁₆˝ base		1 trapezoid
2 × 10 trapezoid	2½˝ tall, 12⁷⁄₁₆˝ base		1 trapezoid
2˝ diamond	2½˝ from side to side		1 diamond
Background			
2˝ triangle	2½˝ tall, 3³⁄₁₆˝ base	1 strip 2½˝* × width of fabric	6 triangles
2 × 4 trapezoid	2½˝ tall, 5½˝ base		1 trapezoid
2 × 8 trapezoid	2½˝ tall, 10⅛˝ base		1 trapezoid

If using a straight ruler to cut the triangles, start with a strip ¼˝ wider than the size listed. The cut size of your triangle will be ¼˝ taller than the cut size in the chart. If you started with a wider strip for straight-ruler cutting the triangles, then trim the remaining strip by ¼˝ before cutting other pieces.

Make the Block

Seam allowances are ¼″ unless otherwise noted. Press all seams open.

1. Sew a background triangle to 2 sides of the feature fabric diamond as shown. Press the seams open after each seam. **FIGS. A–C**

2. Make the remainder of the rows as shown, joining triangles to each end of the trapezoids. **FIG. D**

3. Join the rows. **FIGS. E & F**

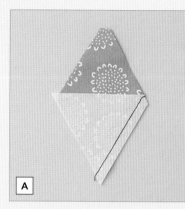

A

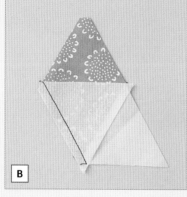

B

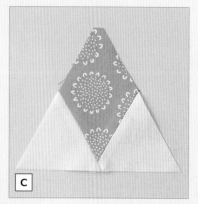

C

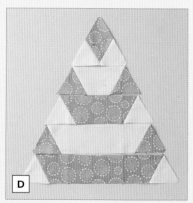

D

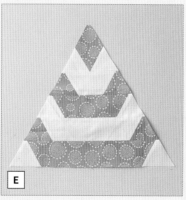

E

Stack the Dishes block

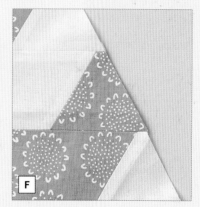

F

Note how the seams cross ¼″ from the raw edge.

Misty Morning

FINISHED BLOCK HEIGHT: 12˝ · **FINISHED QUILT:** 78˝ × 90½˝

As the sun rises in the valley where I live, the mist lifts to reveal a stunning and very long mountain range—the Tararuas. In winter, the peaks are often covered with snow. The combination of the sun, snow, clouds, and forest creates beautiful shadings going from intense violet to light cyan.

For this quilt, I used Blueberry Park fabrics by Karen Lewis for Robert Kaufman Fabrics and combined them with white Kona Cotton. Although this is another rainbow quilt, the effect of the white background is delicate and fresh—quite different from the rich colorings of Caravan (page 41) and After the Storm (page 48).

MATERIALS

Cyan, yellow, orange, pink, magenta, and violet: ⅝ yard

White: 5¾ yards

Binding: ¾ yard

Backing: 7¼ yards

Batting: 86″ × 99″

CUTTING

For step-by-step cutting instructions, see 60° Triangle Basics (page 29), 60° Trapezoid Basics (page 55), and 60° Diamond Basics (page 74). Remember, if you are using a straight ruler to cut the triangles, start with a strip ¼″ wider than the size listed. You may need more strips for cutting directional fabrics or fussy cutting.

SHAPE	CUT SIZE	FIRST, CUT FABRIC STRIPS:	SUBCUT FROM STRIPS:
Cyan, yellow, orange, pink, magenta, and violet: Cut from *each* color:			
2″ triangle	2½″ tall, 3³⁄₁₆″ base	2 strips (12 total) 2½″* × width of fabric	28 triangles (168 total)
2″ diamond	2½″ from side to side	1 strip (6 total) 2½″ × width of fabric	7 diamonds (42 total)
2 × 6 trapezoid	2½″ tall, 7¹³⁄₁₆″ base	2 strips (12 total) 2½″ × width of fabric	7 trapezoids (42 total)
2 × 10 trapezoid	2½″ tall, 12⁷⁄₁₆″ base	3 strips (18 total) 2½″ × width of fabric	7 trapezoids (42 total)

SHAPE	CUT SIZE	FIRST, CUT FABRIC STRIPS:	SUBCUT FROM STRIPS:
White			
2″ triangle	2½″ tall, 3³⁄₁₆″ base	11 strips 2½″* × width of fabric	252 triangles
2 × 4 trapezoid	2½″ tall, 5½″ base	5 strips 2½″ × width of fabric	42 trapezoids
2 × 8 trapezoid	2½″ tall, 10⅛″ base	11 strips 2½″ × width of fabric	42 trapezoids
Angled sashing strips	**Angled sashing strips:** 2½″ tall, 12½″ wide	4 strips 12½″ × width of fabric	From each of 2 strips, mark ⅜″ at the bottom edge. Make a 60° cut slanting up to the right to cut a half-triangle; then cut 9 left parallelograms (18 total) 2½″ wide. At the top right end of the strip, measure ⅜″ and place the ruler vertically to cut a matching half-triangle. Unlike those cut from rectangles, these half-triangles will have blunt tips. Cut the remaining 2 strips in the same manner but in the opposite direction, marking ⅜″ at the top edge and cutting down to the right. 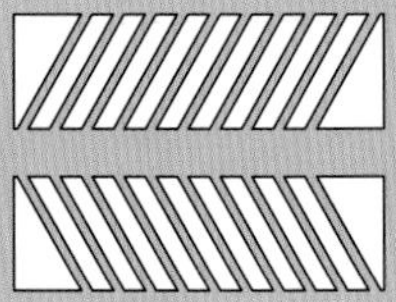
12″ half-triangles	**Half-triangles:** 12½″ tall, 7⅝″ base		
Horizontal sashing strips	2½″ × 69⅞″	10 strips 2½″ × width of fabric	Join the strips; subcut 5 strips 2½″ × 69⅞″.
12″ half-triangles	13³⁄₁₆″ × 7⅝″	1 strip 13³⁄₁₆″ × width of fabric	4 half-triangles from 2 rectangles 13³⁄₁₆″ × 7⅝″. Cut half the rectangles in one direction and half in the opposite. Measure 12½″ up from the bottom and trim the tips to make them match the half-triangles cut previously.
Borders	4½″ wide	9 strips 4½″ × width of fabric	Join the strips; subcut 2 strips 4½″ × 82½″ for the side borders and 2 strips 4½″ × 78″ for the top and bottom borders.
Binding			
		10 strips 2½″ × width of fabric	

*If using a straight ruler to cut the triangles, start with a strip ¼″ wider than the size listed.

Construction

Seam allowances are ¼˝ unless otherwise noted. Press all seams open.

Make the Blocks

Follow the step-by-step instructions for making the Stack the Dishes block (page 80).

1. Make 7 blocks in each of the 6 color combinations, 42 blocks total.

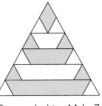

Cyan and white: Make 7.

Yellow and white: Make 7.

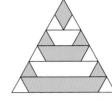

Orange and white: Make 7.

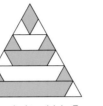

Pink and white: Make 7.

Magenta and white: Make 7.

Violet and white: Make 7.

Quilt Assembly

1. Referring to the quilt assembly diagram, arrange the blocks in rows, placing diagonal sashing strips between the blocks and the half-triangles at the ends of the rows.

2. Sew the blocks, sashings, and triangles together in rows.

3. Join horizontal sashings to the bottom of rows 1–5. Join all the rows together.

4. Add top and bottom borders.

5. Add side borders.

Quilt assembly

Finishing the Quilt

Layer the quilt top with the backing and batting. Baste.

When quilting, think about having a simple repeating design or straight lines in the sashings and a different pattern inside the blocks. See the Stack the Dishes block for another quilting idea.

Misty Morning, 78˝ × 90½˝, designed and pieced by Sheila Christensen, quilted by Sue Burnett

Shadowflower

FINISHED BLOCK HEIGHT: 12˝ • **FINISHED QUILT:** 56˝ × 60½˝

Placing the Stack the Dishes blocks in a kaleidoscope setting reminded me of chrysanthemum flowers with their layers upon layers of crinkled petals. Trips to the garden center are always on the itinerary when I visit my Mum in Kent, known as the Garden of England. We love to take in the bright blooms and then enjoy a cup of tea and a slice of cake together. This quilt makes me think of those precious visits and all the beautiful colors, with the gray blocks representing the dappled light of late afternoon sunshine.

MATERIALS

Violet: ¼ yard

Cyan: ¼ yard

Yellow: ¼ yard

Orange: ⅜ yard

Pink: ⅜ yard

Magenta: ⅜ yard

Gray: ¾ yard

White: 3¼ yards

Binding: ⅝ yard

Backing: 3½ yards

Batting: 63˝ × 69˝

CUTTING

For step-by-step cutting instructions, see 60° Triangle Basics (page 29), 60° Trapezoid Basics (page 55), and 60° Diamond Basics (page 74). Remember, if you are using a straight ruler to cut the triangles, start with a strip ¼˝ wider than the size listed. You may need more strips for cutting directional fabrics or fussy cutting.

NOTE *If you use a straight ruler to cut triangles and other shapes from the same strip, you will need to start with a strip ¾˝ wider than the triangle height and trim it by ¼˝ to cut the remaining shapes.*

SHAPE	CUT SIZE	FIRST, CUT FABRIC STRIPS:	SUBCUT FROM STRIPS:
Violet, cyan, and yellow: Cut from *each* color:			
2˝ triangle	2½˝ tall, 3³⁄₁₆˝ base	1 strip (3 total) 2½˝* × width of fabric	8 triangles (24 total)
2 × 6 trapezoid	2½˝ tall, 7¹³⁄₁₆˝ base		2 trapezoids (6 total)
2˝ diamond	2½˝ from side to side		**2 diamonds (6 total)
2 × 10 trapezoid	2½˝ tall, 12⁷⁄₁₆˝ base	1 strip (3 total) 2½˝ × width of fabric	2 trapezoids (6 total)

SHAPE	CUT SIZE	FIRST, CUT FABRIC STRIPS:	SUBCUT FROM STRIPS:
Orange, pink, and magenta: Cut from *each* color:			
2″ triangle	2½″ tall, 3³⁄₁₆″ base	1 strip (3 total) 2½″* × width of fabric	12 triangles (36 total)
2″ diamond	2½″ from side to side		3 diamonds (9 total)
2 × 6 trapezoid	2½″ tall, 7¹³⁄₁₆″ base	1 strip (3 total) 2½″ × width of fabric	3 trapezoids (9 total)
2 × 10 trapezoid	2½″ tall, 12⁷⁄₁₆″ base	1 strip (3 total) 2½″ × width of fabric	3 trapezoids (9 total)
Gray			
2″ triangle	2½″ tall, 3³⁄₁₆″ base	2 strips 2½″* × width of fabric	40 triangles
2″ diamond	2½″ from side to side	1 strip 2½″ × width of fabric	10 diamonds
2 × 6 trapezoid	2½″ tall, 7¹³⁄₁₆″ base	2 strips 2½″ × width of fabric	10 trapezoids
2 × 10 trapezoid	2½″ tall, 12⁷⁄₁₆″ base	4 strips 2½″ × width of fabric	10 trapezoids
White			
2″ triangle	2½″ tall, 3³⁄₁₆″ base	7 strips 2½″* × width of fabric	150 triangles
2 × 4 trapezoid	2½″ tall, 5½″ base	3 strips 2½″ × width of fabric	25 trapezoids
2 × 8 trapezoid	2½″ tall, 10⅛″ base	7 strips 2½″ × width of fabric	25 trapezoids
12″ triangle	12¾″ tall, 14¾″ base	3 strips 12¾″ × width of fabric	10 triangles
12″ half-triangles	13³⁄₁₆″ × 7⅝″	2 strips 13³⁄₁₆″ × width of fabric	12 half-triangles from 6 rectangles 13³⁄₁₆″ × 7⅝″. Cut half the rectangles in one direction and half in the opposite. You will need only 5 half-triangles in each direction.
Binding			
	7 strips 2½″ × width of fabric		

If using a straight ruler to cut the triangles, start with a strip ¼″ wider than the size listed. The cut size of your triangle will be ¼″ taller than the cut size in the chart. If you started with a wider strip for straight-ruler cutting the triangles, then trim the remaining strip by ¼″ before cutting other pieces.

**To cut 2″ diamonds from directional fabrics, start with a strip 4½″ × width of fabric. See Cutting Upright Diamonds from Directional Fabric (page 76) and Fussy Cutting 60° Diamonds (page 77).*

Construction

Seam allowances are ¼˝ unless otherwise noted. Press all seams open.

Make the Blocks

Follow the step-by-step instructions for making the Stack the Dishes block (page 80).

1. Make blocks in each color combination, as shown.

Violet and white: Make 2.

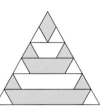

Cyan and white: Make 2.

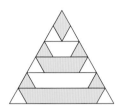

Yellow and white: Make 2.

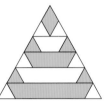

Orange and white: Make 3.

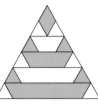

Pink and white: Make 3.

Magenta and white: Make 3.

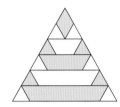

Gray and white: Make 10.

Quilt Assembly

1. Referring to the quilt assembly diagram, arrange the blocks, triangles, and half-triangles as shown.

2. Sew the triangles and blocks together in rows. Sew the rows together.

Quilt assembly

Finishing the Quilt

Quilt and bind the quilt. *Shadowflower* was quilted with a circle pattern inside the blocks, and then Sue treated pairs of white triangles as diamonds for the quilting. See the Stack the Dishes block (page 80) for an additional quilting idea. You could use the same pattern in the background or use this negative space to play with free-motion designs.

Shadowflower, 56″ × 60½″, designed and pieced by Sheila Christensen, quilted by Sue Burnett

LESSON FOUR:
60° PARALLELOGRAM

60° PARALLELOGRAM BASICS

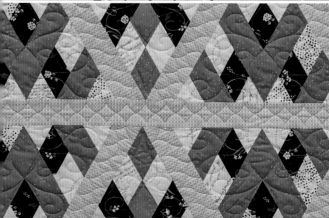

Stretched Diamonds

A parallelogram shape is like a long version of a diamond.

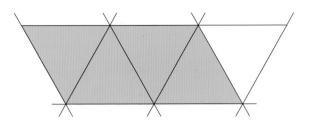

Lean Left or Lean Right

Parallelograms lean either to the left or the right. The only time you *don't* have to worry about which way they are leaning is when you are using a fabric that does not have a right and wrong side, such as a solid.

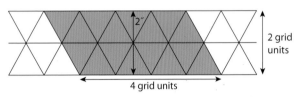

2˝ × 4˝ finished left parallelogram

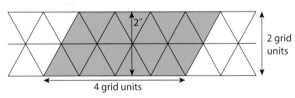

2˝ × 4˝ finished right parallelogram

How Parallelogram Sizes Are Defined

All parallelograms can be measured by their height × the width between the angled sides.

Note: The parallelogram's base—the longest edge—will be a different measurement from the width, but you will not need to use this measurement. Always measure from one angled side to the other.

If the parallelogram is too long for you to measure the width with a 12˝ ruler, then my easy cutting method is to start with a rectangle first and cut angles at both ends. Again, you will not need to measure the base width. The rectangle sizes will be given in the charts.

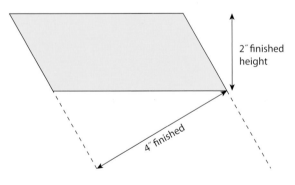

Cutting 60° Parallelograms

1. Start with a strip the same size as the cut height of the parallelogram. For a 2″ × 4″ or 2″ × 6″ parallelogram, start with a 2½″ strip. Cut a 60° angle on the end of the strip, leaning from top left to bottom right for a left parallelogram and in the opposite direction for a right parallelogram. **FIGS. A & B**

2. Place a straight ruler with the cut-size (4½″ or 6½″) ruler line aligned with the angled edge you have just cut. Cut. **FIG. C**

3. Cut multiple parallelograms in the same direction by moving the ruler down the strip and making more cuts. Remember to change the angle to cut shapes in the opposite direction.

TIP You can use the patterns for smaller sizes (page 96) to check that you are cutting the shapes correctly.

Cutting Long Parallelograms

First, cut a rectangle equal to the size listed in the subcutting column of the cutting chart. (Note that the length of this starting rectangle is different from the length of the longest side once you have cut the parallelogram.)

Cut 60° angles off the ends in the same direction, either right or left.

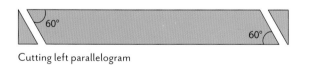

Cutting left parallelogram

Cutting right parallelogram

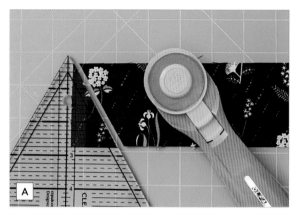

Cutting angle with triangle ruler

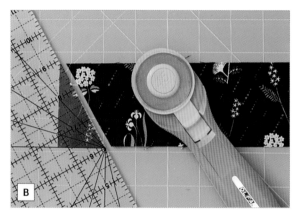

Cutting angle with straight ruler

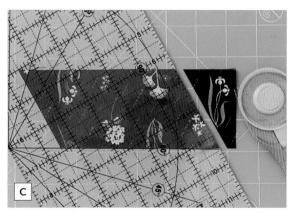

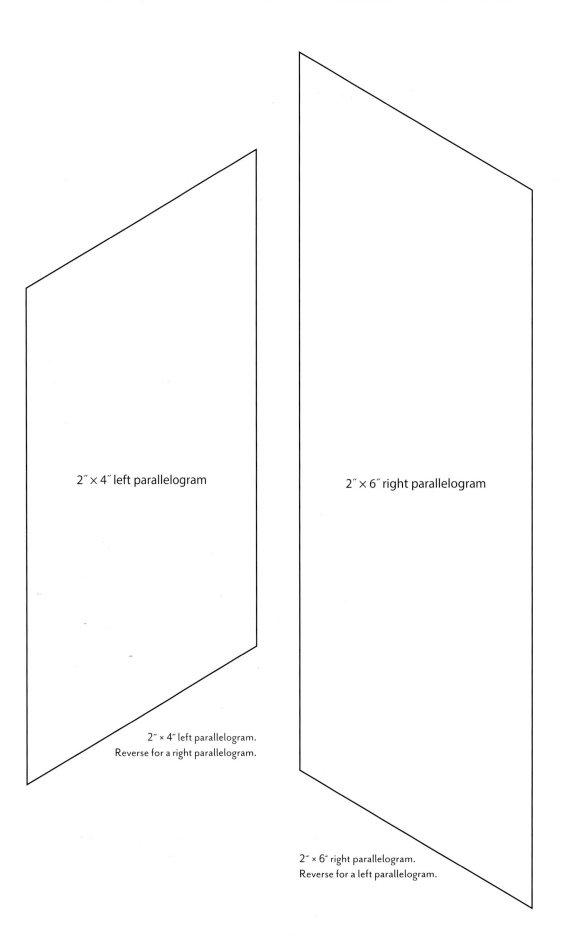

2″ × 4″ left parallelogram

2″ × 6″ right parallelogram

2″ × 4″ left parallelogram.
Reverse for a right parallelogram.

2″ × 6″ right parallelogram.
Reverse for a left parallelogram.

Tie Me in Knots Block

FINISHED BLOCK HEIGHT: 12˝

You won't get tied up in knots making this block if you follow the step-by-step method (page 98). The key is to keep all the pieces laid out next to you as you sew, replacing sections after sewing.

Take a look at *Bejewelled* (page 100) and *Cosmic Rays* (page 106) to see the amazing patterns you can get when this block is combined.

MATERIALS

Fabric 1 (eggshell): 2½˝ × half width of fabric strip

Fabric 2 (teal): 2½˝ × half width of fabric strip

Fabric 3 (blue floral): 2½˝ × width of fabric strip

CUTTING

For step-by-step cutting instructions, see 60° Triangle Basics (page 29), 60° Trapezoid Basics (page 55), 60° Diamond Basics (page 74), and 60° Parallelogram Basics (page 93). Remember, if you are using a straight ruler to cut the triangles, start with a strip ¼˝ wider than the size listed. You may need more strips for cutting directional fabrics or fussy cutting.

SHAPE	CUT SIZE	FIRST, CUT FABRIC STRIPS:	SUBCUT FROM STRIPS:
Fabric 1 (eggshell)			
2˝ triangle	2½˝ tall, 3³⁄₁₆˝ base	1 strip 2½˝* × half width of fabric	4 triangles
2˝ diamond	2½˝ from side to side		4 diamonds
Fabric 2 (teal)			
2˝ diamond	2½˝ from side to side	1 strip 2½˝ × half width of fabric	4 diamonds
Fabric 3 (blue floral)			
2 × 4 trapezoid	2½˝ tall, 5½˝ base	1 strip 2½˝ × width of fabric	2 trapezoids
2˝ × 4˝ left parallelogram	2½˝ tall, 4½˝ wide		1 left parallelogram 4½˝ from side to side
2˝ × 6˝ right parallelogram	2½˝ tall, 6½˝ wide		1 right parallelogram 6½˝ from side to side

*If using a straight ruler to cut the triangles, start with a strip ¼˝ wider than the size listed. The cut size of your triangle will be ¼˝ taller than the cut size in the chart. If you started with a wider strip for straight-ruler cutting the triangles, then trim the remaining strip by ¼˝ before cutting other pieces.

Make the Block

Seam allowances are ¼˝ unless otherwise noted. Press all seams open.

TIP Lay out the pieces before you start. Once a section is sewn, replace it to keep track of which way round the pieces go.

1. Sew a fabric 1 diamond to a fabric 2 diamond. Make 2. **FIG. A**

2. Place these diamonds together to make a four-patch. Join. **FIGS. B & C**

3. Join the 2˝ × 4˝ left parallelogram to the left of the four-patch. Join the 2˝ × 6˝ right parallelogram to the right. **FIG. D**

4. Join a fabric 1 triangle, fabric 2 diamond, and fabric 1 diamond. **FIG. E**

5. Repeat with the pieces in the opposite direction. You will have these sections. **FIG. F**

6. Join fabric 1 triangles to fabric 3 trapezoids. Make 2. **FIG. G**

7. Lay out the parts of the block; then join them together. **FIGS. H & I**

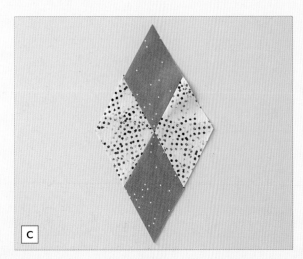

A

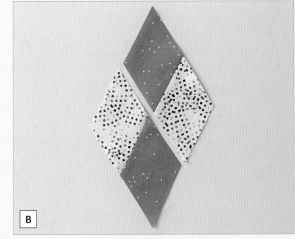

B

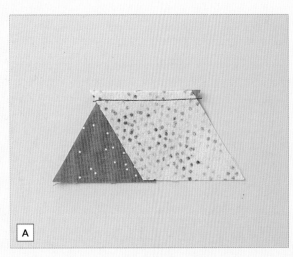

C

D

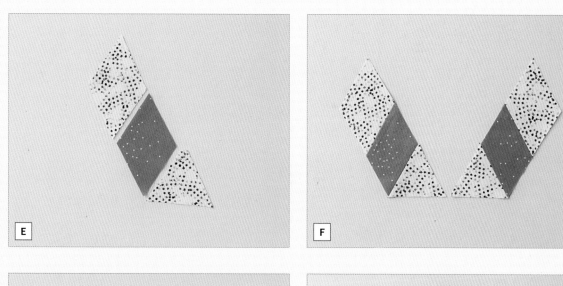

E

F

G

H

I

Tie Me in Knots block

Quilting suggestion for Tie Me in Knots block

Bejewelled

FINISHED BLOCK HEIGHT: 12˝ • **FINISHED QUILT:** 71½˝ × 76½˝

Bejewelled *came about from playing on paper with different configurations for the Tie Me in Knots blocks in a straight setting. The unusual shape made by the blocks makes a change from laying the blocks out in simple rows, and the addition of the blue background triangles emphasizes the shape, which reminds me of a cut jewel. My architect niece helped me figure out how the sashings would work to keep smooth lines at the edges (thanks, Jenny!).*

The fabrics used are mainly from Cotton + Steel Fabrics, with some of Brigitte Heitland's low-volume Modern Background—Paper fabrics from Moda.

MATERIALS

Blue floral: 1½ yards

Teal: 1½ yards

Assorted low-volume prints: ¾ yard

Aqua: 1¼ yards

Light cream print: 1⅞ yards

Binding: ⅝ yard

Backing: 4¾ yards

Batting: 80˝ × 84˝

CUTTING

For step-by-step cutting instructions, see 60° Triangle Basics (page 29), 60° Trapezoid Basics (page 55), 60° Diamond Basics (page 74), and 60° Parallelogram Basics (page 93). Remember, if you are using a straight ruler to cut the triangles, start with a strip ¼˝ wider than the size listed. You may need more strips for cutting directional fabrics or fussy cutting.

SHAPE	CUT SIZE	FOR	FIRST, CUT FABRIC STRIPS:	SUBCUT FROM STRIPS:
Blue floral				
2˝ diamond	2½˝ from side to side	Block A		32 diamonds
2 × 4 trapezoid	2½˝ tall, 5½˝ base	Block B		16 trapezoids
2˝ × 4˝ left parallelogram	2½˝ tall, 4½˝ wide	Block B	8 strips 2½˝ × width of fabric	8 left parallelograms 4½˝ from side to side
2˝ × 6˝ right parallelogram	2½˝ tall, 6½˝ wide	Block B		8 right parallelograms 6½˝ from side to side
14˝ half-triangles	15³⁄₁₆˝ × 8¹³⁄₁₆˝	Setting triangles	1 strip 15³⁄₁₆˝ × width of fabric	8 half-triangles from 4 rectangles 15³⁄₁₆˝ × 8¹³⁄₁₆˝. Cut half the rectangles in one direction and half in the opposite.
Borders	1½˝ wide	Border 2	7 strips 1½˝ × width of fabric	Join the strips; subcut 2 strips 1½˝ × 61⅝˝ for the top and bottom border 2 and 2 strips 1½˝ × 68½˝ for the side border 2.

SHAPE	CUT SIZE	FOR	FIRST, CUT FABRIC STRIPS:	SUBCUT FROM STRIPS:
Teal				
2″ diamond	2½″ from side to side	Block B		32 diamonds
2 × 4 trapezoid	2½″ tall, 5½″ base	Block A		16 trapezoids
2″ 4″ left parallelogram	2½″ tall, 4½″ wide	Block A	8 strips 2½″ × width of fabric	8 left parallelograms 4½″ from side to side
2″ × 6″ right parallelogram	2½″ tall, 6½″ wide	Block A		8 right parallelograms 6½″ from side to side
14″ triangle	14¾″ tall, 17¹⁄₁₆″ base	Setting triangles	2 strips 14¾″ × width of fabric	4 triangles
Assorted low-volume prints				
2″ triangle	2½″ tall, 3³⁄₁₆″ base	Blocks A and B	3 strips 2½″* × width of fabric	64 triangles
2″ diamond	2½″ from side to side	Block B	5 strips 2½″ × width of fabric	64 diamonds
Aqua				
Oversized parallelograms	2½″ tall, 12½″ wide / 1½″ tall, 12½″ wide	Angled sashing strips	2 strips 12½″ × width of fabric	Cut a 60° angle. Cut 8 left parallelograms 2½″ wide and 2 left parallelograms 1½″ wide from 1 strip. Cut the same number of right parallelograms from the second strip. 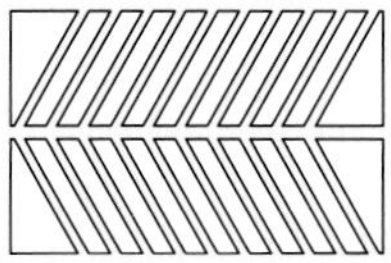
Oversized trapezoid	2½″ tall, 23⅝″ base	Short horizontal sashings	2 strips 2½″ × width of fabric	2 trapezoids from rectangles 2½″ × 23⅝″
Oversized trapezoid	2½″ tall, 40¼″ base	Long horizontal sashings	2 strips 2½″ × width of fabric	Trim the strips to 2½″ × 40¼″. Cut 60° angles off the ends in opposite directions.
Sashing strip	2½″ × 53⅝″	Center horizontal sashing	2 strips 2½″ × width of fabric	Join the strips; subcut 1 strip 2½″ × 53⅝″.

SHAPE	CUT SIZE	FOR	FIRST, CUT FABRIC STRIPS:	SUBCUT FROM STRIPS:
Light cream print				
Borders	4½˝ wide	Borders 1 and 3	14 strips 4½˝ × width of fabric	Join the strips. Subcut 2 strips 4½˝ × 53⅝˝ for the top and bottom border 1 and 2 strips 4½˝ × 66½˝ for the side border 1. Subcut 2 strips 4½˝ × 63⅝˝ for the top and bottom border 3 and 2 strips 4½˝ × 76½˝ for the side border 3.
Binding				
			8 strips 2½˝ × width of fabric	

*If using a straight ruler to cut the triangles, start with a strip ¼˝ wider than the size listed. The cut size of your triangle will be ¼˝ taller than the cut size in the chart.

Construction

Seam allowances are ¼˝ unless otherwise noted. Press all seams open.

Make the Blocks

Follow the step-by-step instructions for making the Tie Me in Knots block (page 97).

Block A and Block B are the same block with the positions of the blue floral and teal fabrics reversed.

1. Make 8 Blocks A, with the blue floral fabric at the top point. **FIG. A**

2. Make 8 Blocks B, with the teal print at the top point. **FIG. B**

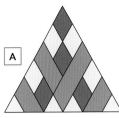

Block A: Make 8.

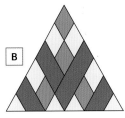

Block B: Make 8.

Quilt Assembly

1. Referring to the quilt assembly diagram, arrange the pieces in rows.

2. To make rows 1 and 4, use 2 Blocks A, 1 Block B, 2 left 2½˝ vertical sashings, 2 right 2½˝ vertical sashings, a short horizontal sashing, 2 large teal triangles, and 2 large blue floral half-triangles. Sew the 3 blocks

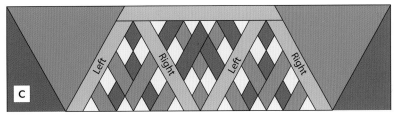

Rows 1 and 4

together first, with the vertical sashings between them and at each end; then add the short horizontal sashing to the top, as shown. Finally, sew the large teal triangle and large blue floral half-triangle to each end, as shown. **FIG. C**

3. To make rows 2 and 3, use 2 Blocks A, 3 Blocks B, 2 left 2½˝ vertical sashings, 2 right 2½˝ vertical sashings, 1 left 1½˝ vertical sashing, 1 right 1½˝ vertical sashing, a long horizontal sashing, and 2 large blue floral half-triangles. Sew the 5 blocks together first, with the 2½˝ vertical sashings between them and the 1½˝ vertical sashings at each end; then add the long horizontal sashing to the top, as shown. Finally, sew the large blue floral half-triangles to each end as shown. **FIG. D**

4. Sew the rows together, adding the center horizontal sashing between rows 2 and 3.

5. Add the top and bottom border 1 and then the side border 1.

6. Repeat Step 5 to add borders 2 and 3.

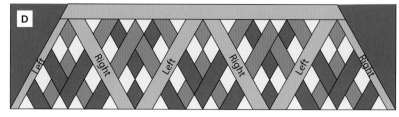

Rows 2 and 3

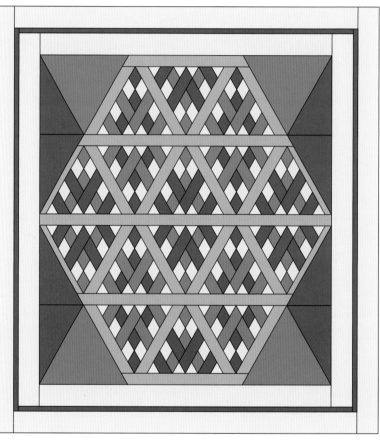

Quilt assembly

Finishing the Quilt

Quilt and bind as desired. Quilting a different pattern in the sashings to the blocks will make the pattern stand out. The background could be quilted with vertical lines ¼˝ apart to make the jewel pop.

Sometimes it's hard to decide on a color for quilting, especially if you are sending your quilt to a longarm quilter. We used a light mint-colored 50-weight Aurifil thread, which blended into all of the colors perfectly and added an extra dimension to the cream backing.

Bejewelled, 71½˝ × 76½˝, designed and pieced by Sheila Christensen, quilted by Sue Burnett

Cosmic Rays

FINISHED BLOCK HEIGHT: 12˝ · **FINISHED QUILT:** 68½˝ × 72˝

When you place triangle blocks in a kaleidoscope setting, stunning effects start to happen. Two different block colorings create the overall effect, and the possibilities for trying out different colorings are virtually endless.

I used Cotton + Steel fabrics for the main colors and then went to my stash of Modern Background—Paper fabrics by Zen Chic for the low-volume prints.

I started by choosing the blue floral and the teal prints to create the star pattern— nothing too busy. You want something that will almost read as a solid, or the pattern will be lost. The background is made up of a combination of low-volume prints. I didn't worry too much about the positions of these in the blocks, but I did end up controlling which print went where when I got onto making the background. There is also a gray print for the rays showing behind the star and aqua for framing the star. The important thing with these fabrics is to choose something that contrasts slightly with your background fabrics but isn't so strong that it overtakes the block patterns.

MATERIALS

Blue floral: ½ yard

Teal: ½ yard

Assorted low-volume prints: ⅝ yard

Cream print: ¾ yard

Aqua print: ⅝ yard

Gray print: ¾ yard

Circle print: 2⅜ yards

Text print: ¾ yard

Binding: ⅝ yard

Backing: 4½ yards

Batting: 76˝ × 80˝

CUTTING

For step-by-step cutting instructions, see 60° Triangle Basics (page 29), 60° Trapezoid Basics (page 55), 60° Diamond Basics (page 74), and 60° Parallelogram Basics (page 93). Remember, if you are using a straight ruler to cut the triangles, start with a strip ¼˝ wider than the size listed. You may need more strips for cutting directional fabrics or fussy cutting.

SHAPE	CUT SIZE	FOR	FIRST, CUT FABRIC STRIPS:	SUBCUT FROM STRIPS:
Blue floral and teal: Cut from *each* color:				
2˝ diamond	2½˝ from side to side	Block A		24 diamonds (48 total)
2 × 4 trapezoid	2½˝ tall, 5½˝ base	Block B	6 strips 2½˝ × width of fabric	12 trapezoids (24 total)
2˝ × 4˝ left parallelogram	2½˝ tall, 4½˝ wide	Block B		6 left parallelograms (12 total) 4½˝ wide from side to side
2˝ × 6˝ right parallelogram	2½˝ tall, 6½˝ wide	Block B		6 right parallelograms (12 total) 6½ wide from side to side

SHAPE	CUT SIZE	FOR	FIRST, CUT FABRIC STRIPS:	SUBCUT FROM STRIPS:
Assorted low-volume prints				
2″ triangle	2½″ tall, 3³⁄₁₆″ base	Blocks A and B	3 strips 2½″* × width of fabric	48 triangles
2″ diamond	2½″ from side to side	Blocks A and B	4 strips 2½″ × width of fabric	48 diamonds
Cream print				
Oversized trapezoid	2½″ tall, 17⅛″ base	Block I	9 strips 2½″ × width of fabric	2 trapezoids from 2½″ × 17⅛″ rectangles
Oversized trapezoid	2½″ tall, 19½″ base	Block I		2 trapezoids from 2½″ × 19½″ rectangles
2″ diamond	2½″ from side to side	Block I		4 diamonds
Oversized parallelograms	2½″ tall	Blocks C and D		4 left and 4 right parallelograms from 2½″ × 16″ rectangles
Oversized trapezoid	2½″ tall, 14¾″ base	Blocks E and F		4 trapezoids from 2½″ × 14¾″ rectangles
2″ × 4″ right parallelogram	2½″ tall, 4½″ wide	Block E		2 right parallelograms 4½″ wide from side to side
2″ × 4″ left parallelogram	2½″ tall, 4½″ wide	Block F		2 left parallelograms 4½″ wide from side to side

SHAPE	CUT SIZE	FOR	FIRST, CUT FABRIC STRIPS:	SUBCUT FROM STRIPS:
Aqua print				
Oversized parallelograms	2½˝ tall	Blocks C and D	7 strips 2½˝ × width of fabric	2 left and 2 right parallelograms from 2½˝ × 16˝ rectangles
Oversized trapezoid	2½˝ tall, 17⅛˝ base	Blocks E and F		4 trapezoids from 2½˝ × 17⅛˝ rectangles
Oversized trapezoid	2½˝ tall, 19½˝ base	Block I		2 trapezoids from 2½˝ × 19½˝ rectangles
Oversized trapezoid	2½˝ tall, 21¾˝ base	Block I		2 trapezoids from 2½˝ × 21¾˝ rectangles. Cut 1 from each of 2 strips; then cut the parallelograms below from the remaining strips.
2˝ × 4˝ right parallelogram	2½˝ tall, 4½˝ wide	Block E		2 right parallelograms 4½˝ wide from side to side
2˝ × 4˝ left parallelogram	2½˝ tall, 4½˝ wide	Block F		2 left parallelograms 4½˝ wide from side to side
Gray print				
Oversized parallelograms	2½˝ tall	Blocks C and G (right) Blocks D and H (left)	8 strips 2½˝ × width of fabric	4 left and 4 right parallelograms from 2½˝ × 20½˝ rectangles. Cut 1 rectangle from each strip; then cut the shapes below from the remaining strips.
Oversized parallelograms	2½˝ tall	Blocks C and D		2 left and 2 right parallelograms from 2½˝ × 16˝ rectangles
Oversized trapezoid	2½˝ tall, 17⅛˝ base	Blocks G and H		4 trapezoids from 2½˝ × 17⅛˝ rectangles
4˝ half-triangles	3˝ × 5³⁄₁₆˝	Blocks E and F	1 strip 3˝ × width of fabric	4 half-triangles from 2 rectangles 3˝ × 5³⁄₁₆˝

SHAPE	CUT SIZE	FOR	FIRST, CUT FABRIC STRIPS:	SUBCUT FROM STRIPS:
Circle print				
 Multi-angle strip	4½″ tall × 20½″	Block G	8 strips 4½″ × width of fabric. Set aside partial strips for borders.	2 rectangles 4½″ × 20½″. Cut a 60° angle from the left end of the strip.  Fold in half lengthwise. Cut a 60° angle on the right end.  Fold. Open the strip. 
 Multi-angle strip	4½″ tall × 20½″	Block H		2 rectangles 4½″ × 20½″. Subcut the rectangles in the same manner as the previous entry, but make the first cut on the right end and the second cut on the folded left end. 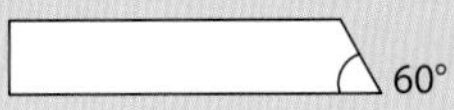 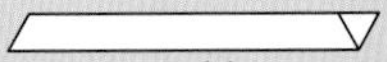 60° Fold.
 Multi-angle strip	4½″ tall × 20½″	Block G		2 rectangles 4½″ × 20½″. Cut a 30° angle on the left and a 60° angle on the right.  60° 30° 60°
 Multi-angle strip	4½″ tall × 20½″	Block H		2 rectangles 4½″ × 20½″. Cut a 60° angle on the left and a 30° angle on the right.  60° 30° 60°
Borders	4½″ wide		4 strips 4½″ × width of fabric	Join a partial strip to each end of a width-of-fabric strip; subcut 2 strips 60½″ for the top and bottom borders and 2 strips 72″ for the side borders.
 12″ triangle	12¾″ tall, 14¾″ base	Blocks G and H	1 strip 12¾″ × width of fabric	4 triangles
 12″ half-triangles	13³⁄₁₆″ × 7⅝″	Blocks C and D	1 strip 7⅝″ × width of fabric	4 half-triangles from 2 rectangles 13³⁄₁₆″ × 7⅝″. Cut half the rectangles in one direction and half in the opposite.

SHAPE	CUT SIZE	FOR	FIRST, CUT FABRIC STRIPS:	SUBCUT FROM STRIPS:
Text print				
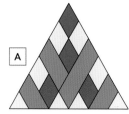 8˝ half-triangles	9³⁄₁₆˝ × 5⁵⁄₁₆˝	Blocks G and H	2 strips 5⁵⁄₁₆˝ × width of fabric	4 half-triangles from 2 rectangles 9³⁄₁₆˝ × 5⁵⁄₁₆˝. Cut 1 rectangle from each strip, and cut 1 in each direction. Set aside the remaining strips.
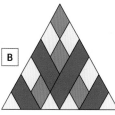 Oversized parallelograms	4½˝ tall	Blocks G and H	2 strips 4½˝ × width of fabric	2 left parallelograms (Block G) and 2 right parallelograms (Block H) from 4½˝ × 21¾˝ rectangles. Cut 2 rectangles from the reserved strips above.
Binding				
8 strips 2½˝ × width of fabric				

If using a straight ruler to cut the triangles, start with a strip ¼˝ wider than the size listed. The cut size of your triangle will be ¼˝ taller than the cut size in the chart.

Construction

Seam allowances are ¼˝ unless otherwise noted.

Press all seams open.

Make the Blocks

Follow the step-by-step instructions for making the Tie Me in Knots block (page 97).

1. Make 6 each of Blocks A and B. **FIGS. A & B**

2. Make 2 each of Blocks C and D, which are mirror images of each other. Start with the circle print triangle. Add the gray, cream, aqua, and another cream parallelogram to complete the blocks. Make sure the top and bottom of the blocks are in a straight line and do not trim. **FIGS. C & D**

3. Make 2 each of Blocks E and F, which are mirror images. Join the long cream and aqua trapezoids; then add the cream and aqua parallelograms to the gray half-triangle. Sew the parallelogram unit to the side of the trapezoid unit, as shown. **FIGS. E & F**

Block A: Make 6.

Block B: Make 6.

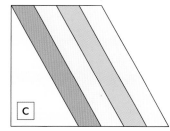
Block C: Make 2.

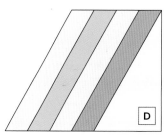
Block D: Make 2.

Block E: Make 2.

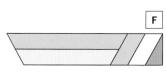
Block F: Make 2.

4. Make 2 each of Blocks G and H, which are mirror images of each other. Start with the 12˝ triangle of the circle print. Join the remaining pieces in the order shown on the diagram. **FIGS. G & H**

5. Make 2 of Block I. Start with a Block B. Join the smaller cream trapezoid to the right side. Add the larger cream trapezoid to the left. Join a cream diamond to the end of each aqua trapezoid. Join the smaller trapezoid of aqua to the right-hand side of the block. Sew the larger trapezoid of aqua to the left-hand side to complete the block. **FIG. I**

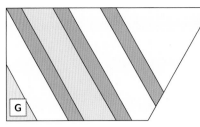

Block G: Make 2.

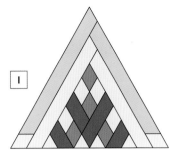

Block I: Make 2.

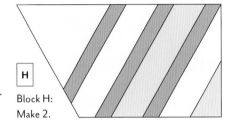

Block H: Make 2.

Quilt Assembly

1. Referring to the quilt assembly diagram, arrange the blocks into rows. **FIG. J**

2. Join Block E to Block G. Join Block F to Block H. Sew the pieced units on either side of Block I. Make 2 for rows 1 and 4. **FIG. K**

3. Join 2 Blocks B and 3 Blocks A in a row, taking note of the positions of the diamonds in the blocks. Add a Block C to the left and a Block D to the right. Make 2 for rows 2 and 3. **FIG. L**

4. Join the rows together.

5. Attach the top and bottom borders; then attach the side borders.

Quilt assembly

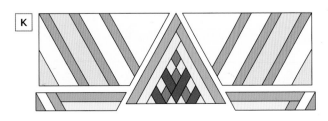

Finishing the Quilt

Layer the quilt top with the backing and batting.

Baste, quilt, and bind

The outlines of the star are a great place to add some detailed quilting.

Cosmic Rays, 68½˝ × 72˝, designed and pieced by Sheila Christensen, quilted by Sue Burnett

LESSON FIVE: HEXAGON

HEXAGON BASICS

Modern Twist on an Old Tradition

Hexagon shapes have been used in patchwork for many centuries. Traditionally they have been pieced by hand, but they are now making a comeback in modern machine-pieced quilts.

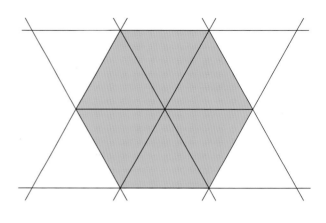

How Hexagon Sizes Are Defined

In this book, hexagons are defined by the measurement from side to side—not the length of the sides, as in English paper piecing. This allows them to be cut easily from a strip. Hexagons measure the same across from any straight edge to the opposite straight edge. This is a great way to check you have cut correctly. A 4˝ finished hexagon should measure 4½˝ from flat side to flat side in any direction.

On a 1˝ triangle grid, a 2˝ hexagon is 2 grid units high and 2 grid units wide.

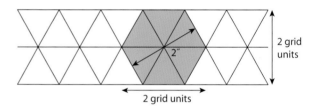

A 4˝ hexagon is 4 grid units high and 4 grid units wide.

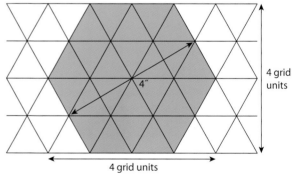

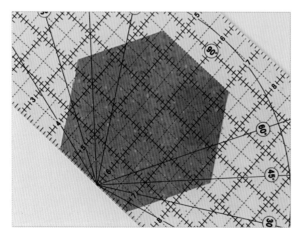

Cutting Hexagons

Using a Triangle Ruler

1. For a 4˝ hexagon, start with a 4½˝ strip. Fold the strip in half lengthwise with the fold at the bottom and place the triangle ruler on the strip. Cut both sides. **FIGS. A & B**

2. Unfold, and voilà! A perfect hexagon! When I figured out how to cut hexagons this way instead of using a pattern and making 6 cuts, I was so excited that I did a little happy dance! **FIG. C**

3. To cut more hexagons, move the ruler along the strip and cut. **FIG. D**

Using a Straight Ruler

You must cut accurately to achieve a perfect hexagon. Cut a test shape first; then check that it measures the correct size in all directions.

1. Start with a rectangle. For a 4˝ finished hexagon, start with a rectangle 4½˝ × 5³⁄₁₆˝. **FIG. E**

2. Fold across the shorter side with the fold at the bottom. Place the 60° line on the fold, with the edge of the ruler touching the outer edge of the fold. Cut. **FIG. F**

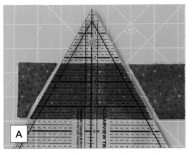
For a point-tip ruler, place the 4½˝ line on the fold.

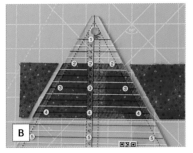
For a blunt-tip ruler, place the 4¼˝ line on the fold.

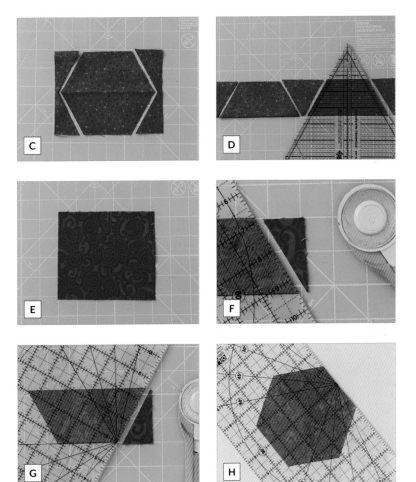

3. Turn the fabric so that the fold is at the top. Place the ruler with the 60° line in the opposite direction, with the edge of the ruler touching the outer edge of the fold at the opposite end of the rectangle. Cut. **FIG. G**

4. Check that the hexagon measures 4½˝ across in each direction. **FIG. H**

Quick Reference: Cutting Hexagons with a Straight Ruler

You must cut accurately to achieve a perfect hexagon. Cut a test shape first; then check that it measures the correct size in all directions.

HEXAGON SIZE	STRIP WIDTH (This is the width from side to side.)	RECTANGLE WIDTH (This is the width from point to point.)
1˝	1½˝	1¾˝
2˝	2½˝	2⅞˝
3˝	3½˝	4¹/₁₆˝
4˝	4½˝	5³/₁₆˝
5˝	5½˝	6⅜˝
6˝	6½˝	7½˝
7˝	7½˝	8¹¹/₁₆˝
8˝	8½˝	9¹³/₁₆˝
9˝	9½˝	11˝
10˝	10½˝	12⅛˝

Fussy Cutting Hexagons

1. Decide how you want to cut the strips. Most fabrics are printed with the pattern direction parallel to the selvage. Be aware of the orientation of the pattern in your fabric before you fussy cut hexagons. **FIG. A**

If you are fussy cutting for quilts where the points are vertical, as for *Watling Street* (page 123), cut the strips parallel to the selvage.

If you want the pattern to be upright when the hexagon is placed with the flat sides top and bottom, as for *Bliss* (page 128), cut the strips perpendicular to the selvage.

2. Find the center of the motif you wish to fussy cut. For a 4˝ hexagon, place the 2¼˝ ruler line on the motif center. **FIG. B**

A

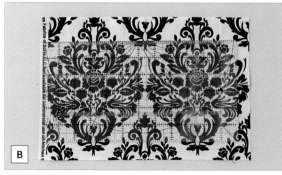

B

3. Cut one edge of the strip. Turn the fabric and place the 4½˝ ruler line on the edge you have just cut. Cut the other edge of the strip. **FIG. C**

4. Fold the fabric in half with the fold on the bottom. **FIG. D**

5. Place the triangle ruler on the strip. For point-tip rulers, put the 4½˝ line on the fold. For blunt-tip rulers, put the 4¼˝ line on the fold. **FIG. E**

6. Cut; then open the hexagon. **FIGS. F & G**

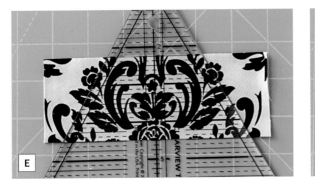

A set of 6 identically cut hexagons would look great in the Tri-Hex blocks for *Bliss* (page 128).

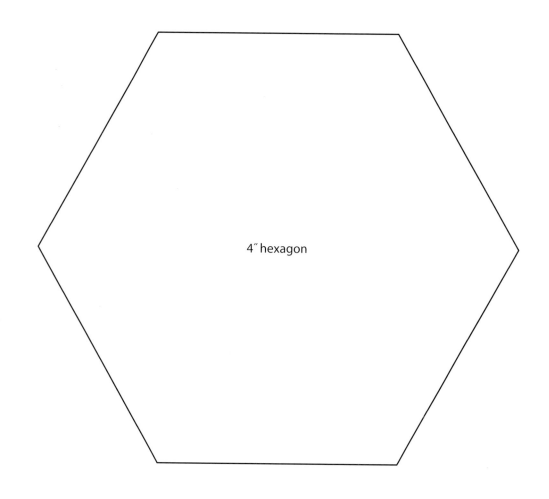

4″ hexagon

Tri-Hex Block

FINISHED BLOCK HEIGHT: 8˝

This is a simple block that makes it easy to machine piece hexagons and combine them in rows, such as in *Watling Street* (page 123), or in a more traditional layout, such as in *Bliss* (page 128).

MATERIALS

Fabric 1 (red): 4½˝ × half width of fabric strip

Fabric 2 (dark gray): 2½˝ × half width of fabric strip

Fabric 3 (cream): 4½˝ × half width of fabric strip

CUTTING

For step-by-step cutting instructions, see 60° Triangle Basics (page 29) and Hexagon Basics (page 115). Remember, if you are using a straight ruler to cut the triangles, start with a strip ¼˝ wider than the size listed. You may need more strips for cutting directional fabrics or fussy cutting.

SHAPE	CUT SIZE	FIRST, CUT FABRIC STRIPS:	SUBCUT FROM STRIPS:
Fabric 1 (red)			
4˝ hexagon	4½˝ tall, 5³⁄₁₆˝ wide	1 strip 4½˝ × half width of fabric	1 hexagon
Fabric 2 (dark gray)			
2˝ triangle	2½˝ tall, 3³⁄₁₆˝ base	1 strip 2½˝* × half width of fabric	2 triangles
Fabric 3 (cream)			
4˝ triangle	4½˝ tall, 5½˝ base	1 strip 4½˝* × half width of fabric	2 triangles

*If using a straight ruler to cut the triangles, start with a strip ¼˝ wider than the size listed.
The cut size of your triangle will be ¼˝ taller than the cut size in the chart.*

Make the Block

Seam allowances are ¼˝ unless otherwise noted. Press all seams open.

1. Attach a fabric 2 triangle to the top of the hexagon.

FIG. A

A

TIP **Joining Triangles to Hexagons**

Line up the triangle with the hexagon so that you can see the same-size tip on either side.

Alternatively, cut the tips off the triangles first with a Corner Cut 60—2-in-1 Sewing Tool (page 26).

2. Join the second fabric 2 triangle to the bottom of the hexagon. **FIG. B**

3. Attach a fabric 3 triangle to the right and left sides of the bottom of the unit. **FIG. C**

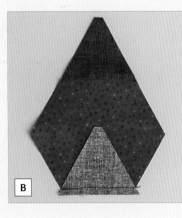

B

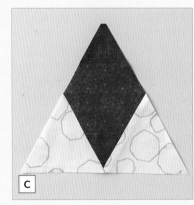

C

Completed Tri-Hex block

Quilting suggestion for Tri-Hex block

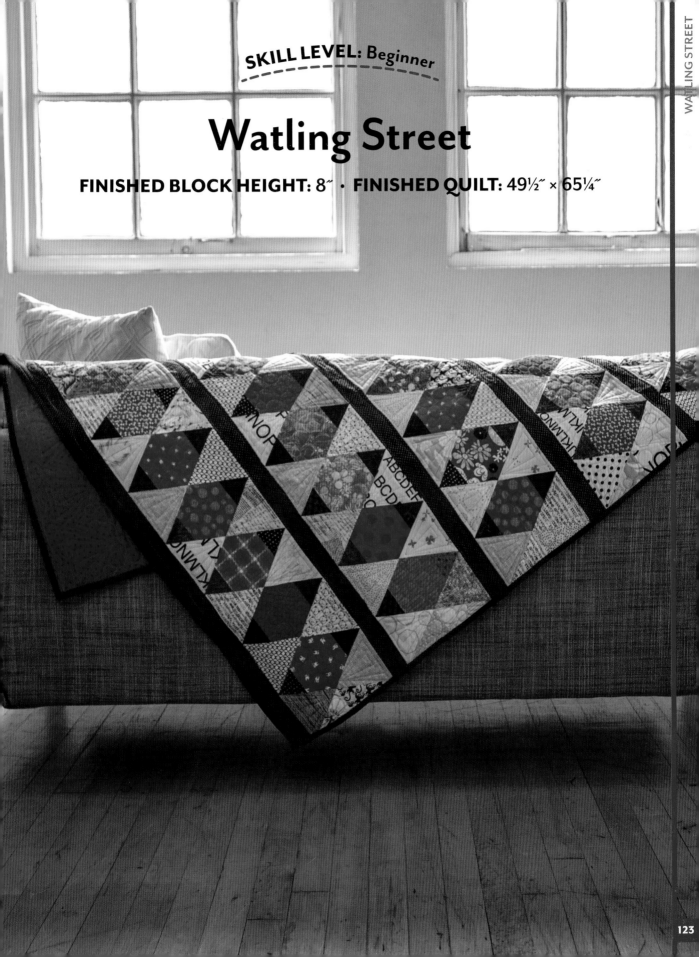

SKILL LEVEL: Beginner

Watling Street

FINISHED BLOCK HEIGHT: 8˝ · **FINISHED QUILT:** 49½˝ × 65¼˝

I love to use a variety of prints in my quilts. This quilt can be thought of as a scrap quilt in a controlled colorway. The effect of using a large number of different fabrics is much more interesting than simply using the same three fabrics throughout the blocks.

The name Watling Street comes from the very straight Roman road that runs through a large part of England. The blocks laid out in rows reminded me of the cobbles that would have been used in the original Roman road.

MATERIALS

Assorted red prints: 10 different fabrics, ⅛ yard of each

Assorted dark gray prints: ½ yard total

Assorted low-volume prints: 1⅞ yards total

Sashing: ¾ yard

Binding: ⅝ yard

Backing: 3¼ yards

Batting: 58″ × 74″

CUTTING

For step-by-step cutting instructions, see 60° Triangle Basics (page 29) and Hexagon Basics (page 115). Remember, if you are using a straight ruler to cut the triangles, start with a strip ¼″ wider than the size listed. You may need more strips for cutting directional fabrics or fussy cutting.

SHAPE	CUT SIZE	FOR	FIRST, CUT FABRIC STRIPS:	SUBCUT FROM STRIPS:
Assorted red prints				
4″ hexagon	4½″ tall, 5³⁄₁₆″ wide	Block A	1 strip 4½″ × width of fabric from *each* fabric	65 hexagons total from all strips. *Note:* The hexagons will point vertically in the quilt. For directional fabric, note your desired pattern direction.
Assorted dark gray prints				
2″ triangle	2½″ tall, 3³⁄₁₆″ base	Block A	6 strips 2½″* × width of fabric	130 triangles

SHAPE	CUT SIZE	FOR	FIRST, CUT FABRIC STRIPS:	SUBCUT FROM STRIPS:
Assorted low-volume prints				
4″ triangle	4½″ tall, 5½″ base	Blocks A, B, and C	12 strips 4½″* × width of fabric	140 triangles
4″ half-triangles	5³⁄₁₆″ × 3″	Blocks B and C	2 strips 3″ × width of fabric	20 half-triangles from 10 rectangles 5³⁄₁₆″ × 3″. Cut half the rectangles in one direction and half in the opposite.
Sashing				
Sashing	2″ × 65¼″	Vertical sashings	10 strips 2″ × width of fabric	Join the strips in pairs and trim to make 6 strips 2″ × 65¼″.
Binding				
7 strips 2½″ × width of fabric				

If using a straight ruler to cut the triangles, start with a strip ¼″ wider than the size listed. The cut size of your triangle will be ¼″ taller than the cut size in the chart. If you started with a wider strip for straight-ruler cutting the triangles, then trim the remaining strip by ¼″ before cutting other pieces.

Construction

Seam allowances are ¼″ unless otherwise noted.

Press all seams open.

Make the Blocks

Follow the step-by-step instructions for making the Tri-Hex block (page 121).

1. Make 65 Tri-Hex blocks. Use different gray and low-volume fabrics in each triangle within the blocks. **FIG. A**

2. Make setting blocks B and C. Join 2 half-triangles; then sew them to one side of a 4″ triangle. **FIGS. B & C**

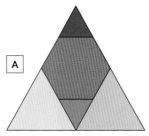
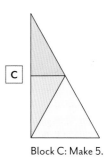

Block A: Make 65.

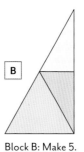

Block B: Make 5.

Block C: Make 5.

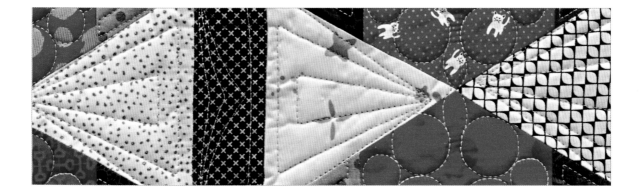

Quilt Assembly

1. Referring to the quilt assembly diagram, arrange the quilt in columns with 13 blocks per column. Add setting blocks B and C at either end.

2. Sew the columns together; then join the sashing strips and columns together.

Quilt assembly

Finishing the Quilt

Quilt and bind as desired. Quilting the triangles and hexagons with different patterns emphasizes the visual difference between the different elements in the design. See the Tri-Hex block (page 121) for an additional quilting idea.

Watling Street, 49½˝ × 65¼˝, designed and pieced by Sheila Christensen, quilted by Sue Burnett

Bliss

FINISHED BLOCK HEIGHT: 8˝ • **FINISHED QUILT:** 74½˝ × 80½˝

*Find your bliss playing with your fabric stash and combining colors to
make the blocks for this scrappy quilt. Vary the placement of the red, gray,
and low-volume fabrics to make your own unique composition.*

*The Tri-Hex blocks in a kaleidoscope setting create hexagonal "blocks" that are
reminiscent of a traditional Grandmother's Flower Garden quilt. By joining sets
of three Tri-Hex blocks into half-hexagons and joining the full hexagons only
when the rows are assembled, the sewing becomes straightforward.*

MATERIALS

*Because this quilt is quite scrappy, the quantities for each color are approximate. Use what you have, and add in those
irresistible fabrics that you find in your local quilt shop.*

Assorted red and black prints: 2⅞ yards total for
hexagons (at least ¼ yard *each* of 11 fabrics)

Assorted black, gray, and white prints: 2⅞ yards total for
4˝ triangles (at least 9˝ × width of fabric *each* of 11 fabrics)

Assorted black, gray, low-volume, and red prints:
1⅝ yards total for 2˝ triangles (at least 5˝ × width of fabric
each of 11 fabrics)

Assorted light gray and low-volume prints: 1⅜ yards
total for background and half-triangles

Binding: ¾ yard

Backing: 7 yards

Batting: 83˝ × 89˝

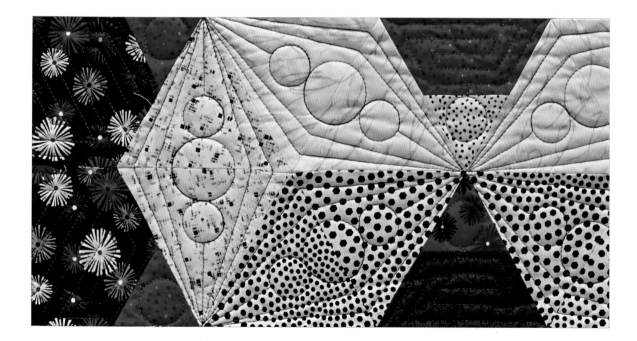

ALTERNATIVE BLOCK LAYOUTS

These are just some of the combinations in my quilt. Have fun experimenting with your own blocks.

Tri-Hex block using a red hexagon, 2˝ black triangles, and 4˝ white triangles

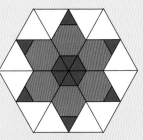

Hexagon assembly using 6 matching blocks

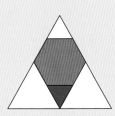

Tri-Hex block with a 2˝ white triangle at the tip

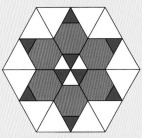

Hexagon assembly with alternating color placement for a different effect

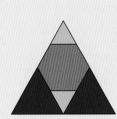

Tri-Hex block using 2˝ gray triangles and 4˝ black triangles

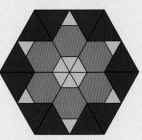

Hexagon assembly using 6 matching blocks in red, gray, and black

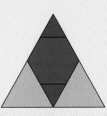

Tri-Hex block with a black hexagon, 2˝ red triangles, and 4˝ gray triangles

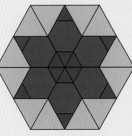

Hexagon assembly using 6 matching blocks

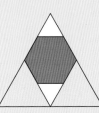

Tri-Hex block with a red hexagon, 2˝ white triangles, and 4˝ gray triangles

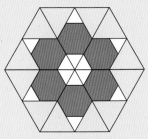

Hexagon assembly using 6 matching blocks

CUTTING

For step-by-step cutting instructions, see 60° Triangle Basics (page 29) and Hexagon Basics (page 115). Remember, if you are using a straight ruler to cut the triangles, start with a strip ¼˝ wider than the size listed. You may need more strips for cutting directional fabrics or fussy cutting.

Cut the pieces for 1 set of blocks (a hexagon assembly) at a time. Each assembly contains 6 blocks, which can be the same, or you can alternate blocks, making 3 of each. See Alternative Block Layouts (previous page) for examples of block colorings.

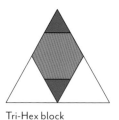

Tri-Hex block

SHAPE	CUT SIZE	FOR	FIRST, CUT FABRIC STRIPS:	SUBCUT FROM STRIPS:
Hexagon assemblies Cut the following set of pieces for *each* hexagon assembly. You will need 22 sets.				
Assorted red and black prints				
4˝ hexagon	4½˝ tall, 5³⁄₁₆˝ wide	1 hexagon assembly	1 strip (22 total) 4½˝ × width of fabric	6 hexagons (132 total)
Assorted black, gray, and white prints				
4˝ triangle	4½˝ tall, 5½˝ base	1 hexagon assembly	1 strip (22 total) 4½˝* × width of fabric	12 triangles (264 total)
Assorted black, gray, low-volume, and red prints				
2˝ triangle	2½˝ tall, 3³⁄₁₆˝ base	1 hexagon assembly	1 strip (22 total) 2½˝* × width of fabric	12 triangles (264 total)
Background and setting triangles				
Assorted light gray and low-volume prints				
8˝ triangle	8½˝ tall, 10⅛˝ base	Setting triangles	8½˝* strips	18 triangles
8˝ half-triangles	9³⁄₁₆˝ × 5⁵⁄₁₆˝	Setting half-triangles	Cut rectangles from assorted fabrics.	20 half-triangles from 10 rectangles 9³⁄₁₆˝ × 5⁵⁄₁₆˝. Cut half the rectangles in one direction and half in the opposite.
Binding				
9 strips 2½˝ × width of fabric				

*If using a straight ruler to cut the triangles, start with a strip ¼˝ wider than the size listed. The cut size of your triangle will be ¼˝ taller than the cut size in the chart.

Construction

Seam allowances are ¼˝ unless otherwise noted. Press all seams open.

Make the Blocks

Follow the step-by-step instructions for making the Tri-Hex block (page 121).

1. Make 22 sets of 6 Tri-Hex blocks using each color combination that you select.

2. Sew the blocks for each hexagon assembly together in sets of 3 to make half-hexagons. Pin the halves together, but do not sew the center seam. **FIG. A**

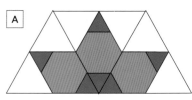

Half-hexagon assembly

Quilt Assembly

1. Referring to the quilt assembly diagram, arrange the full hexagon assemblies as shown. Place the background triangles at the top and bottom and the setting half-triangles at each side.

2. Remove the pins holding the half-hexagon assemblies together. Now you will be able to sew the half-hexagons and setting pieces together in rows. Join the rows together to complete the quilt.

TIP Once you are happy with your layout, label each row with a number. Pick up one row at a time, sew, and replace on your design wall.

Quilt assembly

Finishing the Quilt

Quilt and bind the quilt as desired. For quilting, treat the hexagon assemblies as 1 block. See the Tri-Hex block (page 121) for an additional quilting idea.

Bliss, 74½˝ × 80½˝, designed and pieced by Sheila Christensen, quilted by Sue Burnett

LESSON SIX: 60° JEWEL

60° JEWEL BASICS

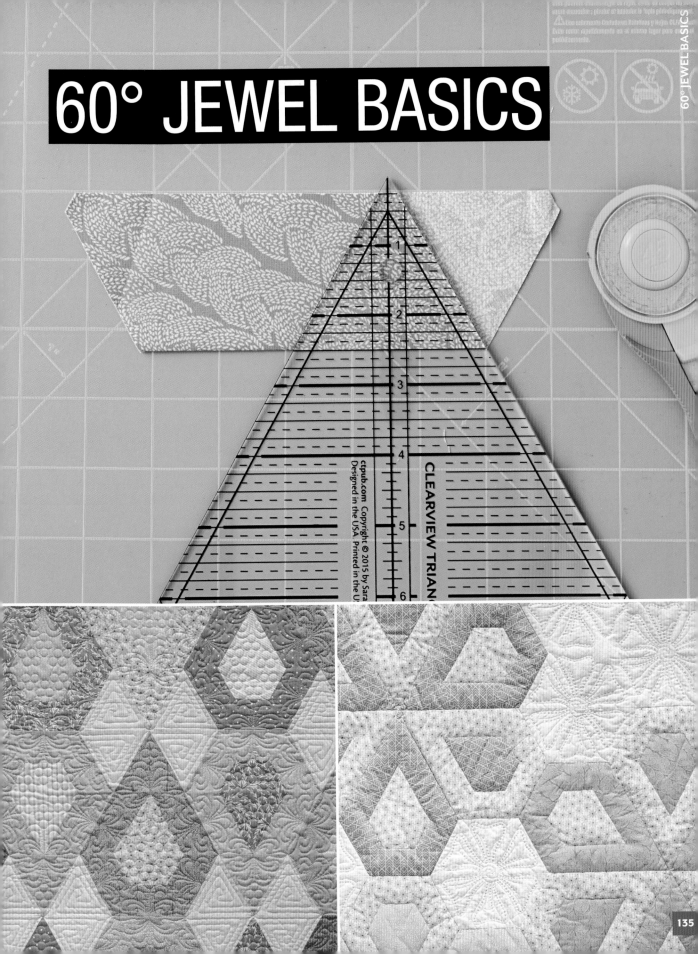

Ring the Changes

Jewel shapes make an interesting change from the regular triangles and hexagons. A jewel can be thought of as a diamond that has lost a triangle or a hexagon with an extra triangle on one side.

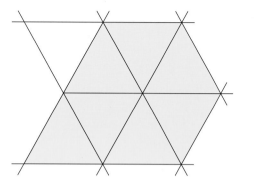

How Jewel Sizes Are Defined

Jewels are cut from diamonds and are defined by the size of diamond.

On a 1˝ triangle grid, a 4˝ jewel is 4 grid units high × 4 grid units wide on its widest side.

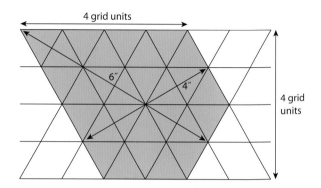

Cutting 60° Jewels

Cutting a jewel starts with cutting a diamond. There are two ways to cut a diamond—with the fabric pattern running parallel to the angle of the diamond or with the pattern running straight up and down, from point to point. See 60° Diamond Basics (page 74).

This jewel shape has the stripe running across the block at an angle. To achieve this look with a directional fabric, see Cutting Diamonds from Nondirectional Fabric (page 75).

Here the stripe has been cut so that it will run vertically in the block. To achieve this look with a directional fabric, see Cutting Upright Diamonds from Directional Fabric (page 76).

1. Cut a diamond. Fold the diamond in half with the straight sides together. FIG. A

2. Position the ruler as shown and cut off the triangle that is showing. The ruler type does not matter; you are just cutting even with the edge of the folded shape. FIG. B

3. The jewel shape is complete. FIG. C

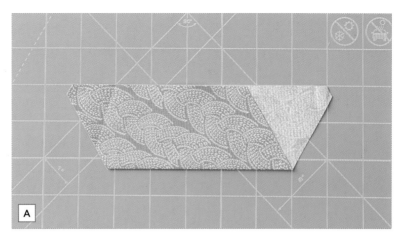

A

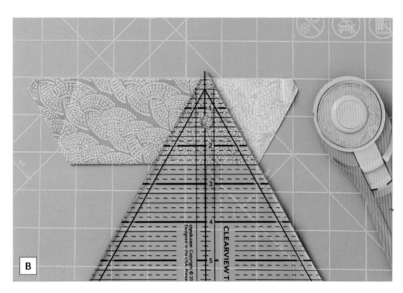

B

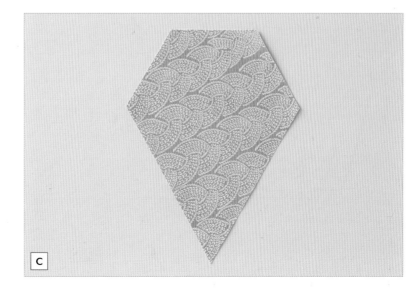

C

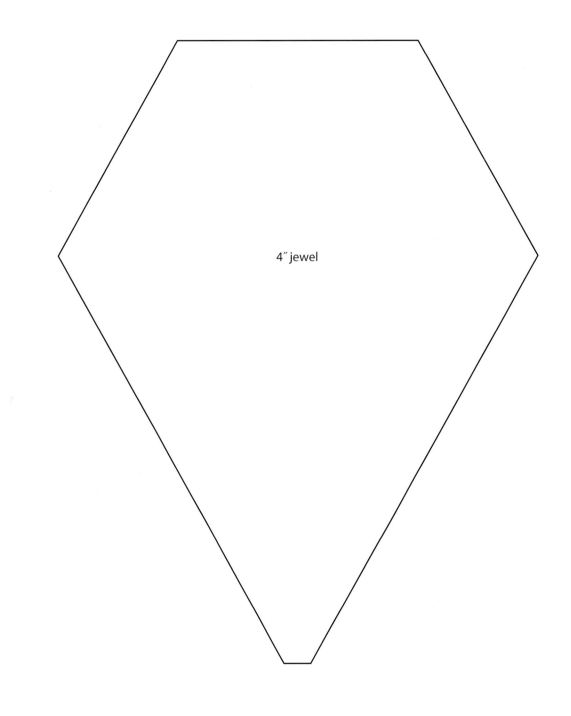

4″ jewel

Petal Block

FINISHED BLOCK HEIGHT: 12˝

This pretty block has a framed jewel shape. When combined in a kaleidoscope setting, as in *Apple Blossom Time*, the blocks look like petals. In *Patisserie*, the blocks are in a straight setting that can look like dewdrops.

MATERIALS

Fabric 1 (coral): 6½˝ × half width of fabric strip for jewel

Fabric 2 (floral): 4½˝ × width of fabric strip for triangle and trapezoids

Fabric 3 (background): 4½˝ × half width of fabric strip for triangles

CUTTING

For step-by-step cutting instructions, see *60° Triangle Basics* (page 29), *60° Trapezoid Basics* (page 55), and *60° Jewel Basics* (page 135). Remember, if you are using a straight ruler to cut the triangles, start with a strip ¼˝ wider than the size listed. You may need more strips for cutting directional fabrics or fussy cutting.

SHAPE	CUT SIZE	FIRST, CUT FABRIC STRIPS:	SUBCUT FROM STRIPS:
Fabric 1 (coral)			
4˝ jewel	4½˝ from side to side	4½˝ × 8½˝ rectangle	1 jewel, subcut from 1 diamond 4½˝ from side to side. See note at end of chart.
Fabric 2 (floral)			
4˝ triangle	4½˝ tall, 5½˝ base	1 rectangle 4½˝* × 5½˝	1 triangle
2 × 4 trapezoid	2½˝ tall, 5½˝ base	Trim remaining strip to 2½˝ × width of fabric.	4 trapezoids
2 × 6 trapezoid	2½˝ tall, 7¹³⁄₁₆˝ base		1 trapezoid
Fabric 3 (background)			
4˝ triangle	4½˝ tall, 5½˝ base	4½˝* × half width of fabric	2 triangles

*If using a straight ruler to cut the triangles, start with a strip ¼˝ wider than the size listed. The cut size of your triangle will be ¼˝ taller than the cut size in the chart.

Note: For using directional fabrics in diamonds and jewels, as I did, start with a rectangle 8½˝ × 6½˝. See Cutting Upright Diamonds from Directional Fabric (page 76) and Fussy Cutting 60° Diamonds (page 77).

Make the Block

Seam allowances are ¼˝ unless otherwise noted. Press all seams open.

1. Join a 2 × 4 trapezoid to the bottom right of the jewel shape. **FIG. A**

2. Join a 2 × 4 trapezoid to the bottom left. **FIG. B**

3. Join a 2 × 4 trapezoid to the top left and another 2 × 4 trapezoid to the top right. **FIG. C**

4. Join a 2 × 6 trapezoid to the top. **FIG. D**

5. Join the fabric 2 triangle to the bottom. **FIG. E**

6. Join a fabric 3 triangle to the top left and top right to complete the block. **FIG. F**

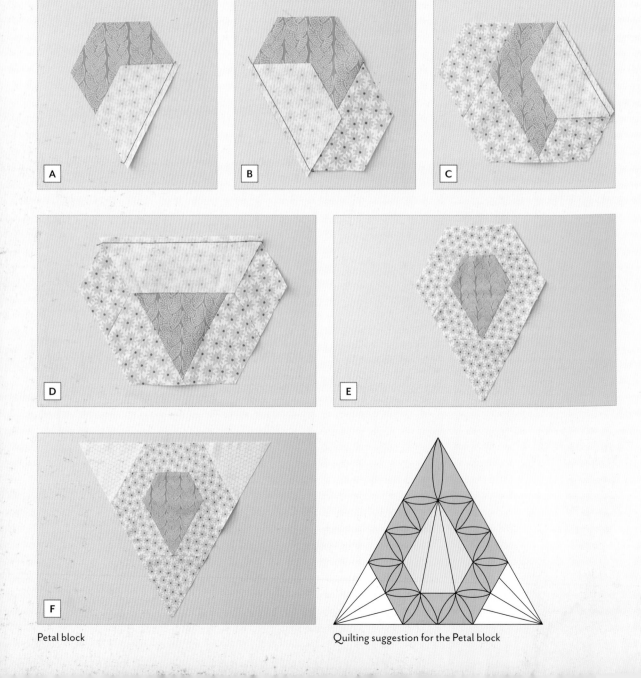

Petal block

Quilting suggestion for the Petal block

SKILL LEVEL: Beginner to intermediate

Patisserie

FINISHED BLOCK HEIGHT: 12˝ • **FINISHED QUILT:** 70˝ × 72½˝

Wouldn't you love to be looking in at the window of a French patisserie shop, eyeing up the delicious colors of the macaroons? This quilt is a great chance to use up your scraps or include some pretty cotton prints saved from little dresses or shirts to make a sweet memory quilt.

For this quilt, pick contrasting hues (opposites on the color wheel). I used teals and aquas for one set of blocks and corals and pinks for the alternate columns. Add interest by mixing different types of prints—spots, stripes, florals, and plaids. I used two different cream prints for this purpose.

MATERIALS

Note: *If any of your fabrics are directional, increase the quantity to ⅝ yard.*

Light teal and aqua: ½ yard *each of* 4 different prints

Medium teal and aqua: ½ yard *each of* 4 different prints

Light coral and pink: ½ yard *each of* 3 different prints

Medium coral and pink: ½ yard *each of* 3 different prints

Cream: 2⅝ yards for blocks and background

Binding: ⅝ yard

Backing: 4½ yards

Batting: 78˝ × 81˝

CUTTING

For step-by-step cutting instructions, see 60° Triangle Basics (page 29), 60° Trapezoid Basics (page 55), and 60° Jewel Basics (page 135). Remember, if you are using a straight ruler to cut the triangles, start with a strip ¼˝ wider than the size listed. You may need more strips for cutting directional fabrics or fussy cutting.

SHAPE	CUT SIZE	FIRST, CUT FABRIC STRIPS:	SUBCUT FROM STRIPS:
All teal/aqua and pink/coral: Cut from *each* of 14 prints:			
4˝ triangle	4½˝ tall, 5½˝ base		3 triangles (42 total)
4˝ jewel	4½˝ from side to side	1 strip (8 total) 4½˝** × width of fabric	3 jewels (42 total), subcut from 3 diamonds 4½˝ from side to side. See note at end of chart.
2 × 4 trapezoid	2½˝ tall, 5½˝ base	3 strips 2½˝ × width of fabric	12 trapezoids (168 total)
2 × 6 trapezoid	2½˝ tall, 7¹³⁄₁₆˝ base		3 trapezoids (42 total)

SHAPE	CUT SIZE	FIRST, CUT FABRIC STRIPS:	SUBCUT FROM STRIPS:
Cream			
▲ 4″ triangle	4½″ tall, 5½″ base	7 strips 4½″* × width of fabric	84 triangles
▲ 12″ triangle	12½″ tall, 14¾″ base	3 strips 12½″* × width of fabric	12 triangles
◢◣ 12″ half-triangles	13³⁄₁₆″ × 7⅝″	Cut rectangles from assorted fabrics.	12 half-triangles from 6 rectangles 13³⁄₁₆″ × 7⅝″. Cut half the rectangles in one direction and the other half in the opposite.
Binding			
8 strips 2½″ × width of fabric			

*If using a straight ruler to cut the triangles, start with a strip ¼″ wider than the size listed. The cut size of your triangle will be ¼″ taller than the cut size in the chart.

**For cutting diamonds from directional fabrics, start with a strip 8½″ × width of fabric. See Cutting Upright Diamonds from Directional Fabric (page 76) and Fussy Cutting 60° Diamonds (page 77).

Construction

Seam allowances are ¼″ unless otherwise noted.

Press all seams open.

Make the Blocks

Follow the step-by-step instructions for making the Petal block (page 139).

1. Make 24 blocks in the teal and aqua prints. Make 12 blocks with light prints at the center and medium prints around the outer edge; reverse the placement for the remaining 12 blocks. Mix and match prints to make a variety of different color combinations. **FIGS. A & B**

2. Make 18 blocks in the pink and coral prints. Make 9 with light prints at the center and the remaining 9 with medium prints at the center. Mix and match prints to make a variety of different color combinations. **FIGS. C & D**

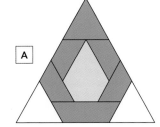

A

Block with light center:
Make 12.

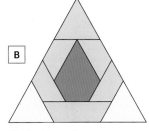

B

Block with medium center:
Make 12.

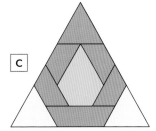

C

Block with light center:
Make 9.

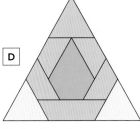

D

Block with medium center:
Make 9.

Quilt Assembly

1. Referring to the quilt assembly diagram, arrange the blocks in 6 rows of 7 blocks each, starting with a teal/aqua block and alternating with the pink/coral blocks.

2. Once you are happy with the arrangement, sew the rows together, adding cream background triangles and half-triangles to the ends of each row.

3. Sew the rows together.

Quilt assembly

Finishing the Quilt

Quilt and bind the quilt as desired. Sue quilted *Patisserie* using a pattern that makes me think of whipped cream, with lots of bubbles and flourishes. See the Petal block (page 139) for another quilting idea.

Patisserie, 70˝ × 72½˝, designed and pieced by Sheila Christensen, quilted by Sue Burnett

Apple Blossom Time

FINISHED BLOCK HEIGHT: 12˝ · **FINISHED QUILT:** 61˝ × 72½˝

The Petal block combines to make flowers that remind me of the spring blossoms on the apple tree in my garden. Alternate the block colorings inside each flower to make the petals stand out. There are two additional blocks in this quilt that are made with 4˝ diamonds.

Take a look at the quilting detail at the end of the project and you will see how I added my own personal touch to the computerized longarm quilting.

MATERIALS

Note: *If you are using directional fabric, allow extra for cutting diamonds and jewels.*

Dark pink: ¾ yard

Medium coral: ½ yard

Light coral: ½ yard

Floral: 1⅜ yards

Yellow: ½ yard

Cream: 2⅜ yards

Binding: ⅝ yard

Backing: 4 yards

Batting: 69˝ × 81˝

CUTTING

For step-by-step cutting instructions, see 60° Triangle Basics (page 29), 60° Trapezoid Basics (page 55), and 60° Jewel Basics (page 135). Remember, if you are using a straight ruler to cut the triangles, start with a strip ¼˝ wider than the size listed. You may need more strips for cutting directional fabrics or fussy cutting.

SHAPE	CUT SIZE	FIRST, CUT FABRIC STRIPS:	SUBCUT FROM STRIPS:
Dark pink			
4˝ triangle	4½˝ tall, 5½˝ base	1 strip 4½˝** × width of fabric	3 triangles
4˝ diamond	4½˝ from side to side		1 diamond 4½˝ from side to side
4˝ jewel	4½˝ from side to side		3 jewels, subcut from 3 diamonds 4½˝ from side to side. See note at end of chart.
2 × 4 trapezoid	2½˝ tall, 5½˝ base	2 strips 2½˝ × width of fabric	12 trapezoids
2 × 6 trapezoid	2½˝ tall, 7¹³⁄₁₆˝ base		3 trapezoids
Borders	2½˝ wide	4 strips 2½˝ × width of fabric	Join the strips; subcut 1 strip 66½˝ for border 7 and 1 strip 57˝ for border 8.

SHAPE	CUT SIZE	FIRST, CUT FABRIC STRIPS:	SUBCUT FROM STRIPS:
Medium coral			
4″ triangle	4½″ tall, 5½″ base	1 strip 4½″** × width of fabric	3 triangles
4″ diamond	4½″ from side to side		1 diamond 4½″ from side to side
4″ jewel	4½″ from side to side		3 jewels, subcut from 3 diamonds 4½″ from side to side. See note at end of chart.
2 × 4 trapezoid	2½″ tall, 5½″ base	2 strips 2½″ × width of fabric	12 trapezoids
2 × 6 trapezoid	2½″ tall, 7¹³⁄₁₆″ base		3 trapezoids
Light coral			
4″ triangle	4½″ tall, 5½″ base	1 strip 4½″** × width of fabric	3 triangles
4″ diamond	4½″ from side to side		2 diamonds 4½″ from side to side
4″ jewel	4½″ from side to side		3 jewels, subcut from 3 diamonds 4½″ from side to side. See note at end of chart.
2 × 4 trapezoid	2½″ tall, 5½″ base	2 strips 2½″ × width of fabric	12 trapezoids
2 × 6 trapezoid	2½″ tall, 7¹³⁄₁₆″ base		3 trapezoids
Floral			
4″ triangle	4½″ tall, 5½″ base	2 strips 4½″** × width of fabric	9 triangles
4″ jewel	4½″ from side to side		9 jewels, subcut from 9 diamonds 4½″ from side to side. See note at end of chart.
2 × 4 trapezoid	2½″ tall, 5½″ base	6 strips 2½″ × width of fabric	36 trapezoids
2 × 6 trapezoid	2½″ tall, 7¹³⁄₁₆″ base		9 trapezoids
Borders	4½″ wide	4 strips 4½″ × width of fabric	Join the strips; subcut 1 strip 68½″ for border 9 and 1 strip 61¼″ for border 10.
Yellow			
4″ diamond	4½″ from side to side	1 strip 4½″ × width of fabric	2 diamonds 4½″ from side to side
Borders	2½″ wide	3 strips 2½″ × width of fabric	Join the strips; subcut 1 strip 60½″ for border 3 and 1 strip 51″ for border 4.

SHAPE	CUT SIZE	FIRST, CUT FABRIC STRIPS:	SUBCUT FROM STRIPS:
Cream			
4″ triangle	4½″ tall, 5½″ base	4 strips 4½″* × width of fabric	42 triangles
12″ half-triangles	7⅝″ × 13³⁄₁₆″	1 strip 13³⁄₁₆″ × width of fabric	8 half-triangles from 4 rectangles 13³⁄₁₆″ × 7⅝″. Cut half the rectangles in one direction and half in the opposite.
12″ triangle	12¾″ tall, 14¾″ base	1 strip 12¾″* × width of fabric	4 triangles
Borders	6½″ wide	3 strips 6½″ × width of fabric	Join the strips; subcut 2 strips 49″ for borders 1 and 2.
Borders	4½″ wide	3 strips 4½″ × width of fabric	Join the strips; subcut 1 strip 62½″ for border 5 and 1 strip 55″ for border 6.
Binding			
8 strips 2½″ × width of fabric			

*If using a straight ruler to cut the triangles, start with a strip ¼″ wider than the size listed. The cut size of your triangle will be ¼″ taller than the cut size in the chart. If you started with a 4¾″ strip for straight-ruler cutting the triangles, then trim the remaining strip to 4½″ before cutting other pieces.

**For using directional fabrics in diamonds and jewels, start with a strip 8½″ × width of fabric. See Cutting Upright Diamonds from Directional Fabric (page 76) and Fussy Cutting 60° Diamonds (page 77).

Construction

Seam allowances are ¼″ unless otherwise noted. Press all seams open.

Make the Blocks

Follow the step-by-step instructions for making the Petal block (page 139). The fabrics for each set of blocks are the same but used in different locations.

1. Make 6 blocks with the dark pink and floral fabrics, 3 with dark pink jewels and 3 with floral jewels. **FIGS. A & B**

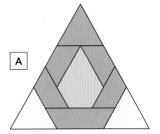

Block with floral jewel: Make 3.

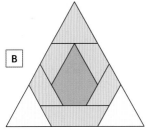

Block with dark pink jewel: Make 3.

2. Make 6 blocks with the medium coral and floral fabrics, 3 with medium coral jewels and 3 with floral jewels. **FIGS. C & D**

3. Make 6 blocks with light coral and floral fabrics, 3 with light coral jewels and 3 with floral jewels. **FIGS. E & F**

4. Make 1 triangle block using 3 cream triangles, 1 light coral diamond, 1 medium coral diamond, and 1 yellow diamond. **FIG. G**

5. Make 1 triangle block using 3 cream triangles, 1 light coral diamond, 1 dark pink diamond, and 1 yellow diamond. **FIG. H**

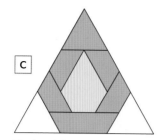

Block with floral jewel: Make 3.

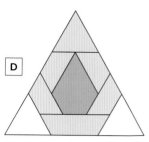

Block with medium coral jewel: Make 3.

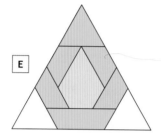

Block with floral jewel: Make 3.

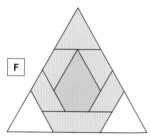

Block with light coral jewel: Make 3.

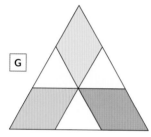

Light coral, medium coral, and yellow: Make 1.

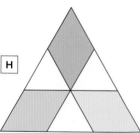

Light coral, dark pink, and yellow: Make 1.

Quilt Assembly

1. Referring to the quilt assembly diagram, arrange the blocks and lay out the background triangles and half-triangles to complete the inner section of the quilt top.

2. Add cream borders 1 and 2 to the top and bottom.

3. Add yellow borders 3 and 4 to the left and top.

4. Add cream borders 5 and 6 to the left and top.

5. Add dark pink borders 7 and 8 to the right and bottom.

6. Add floral borders 9 and 10 to the right and bottom.

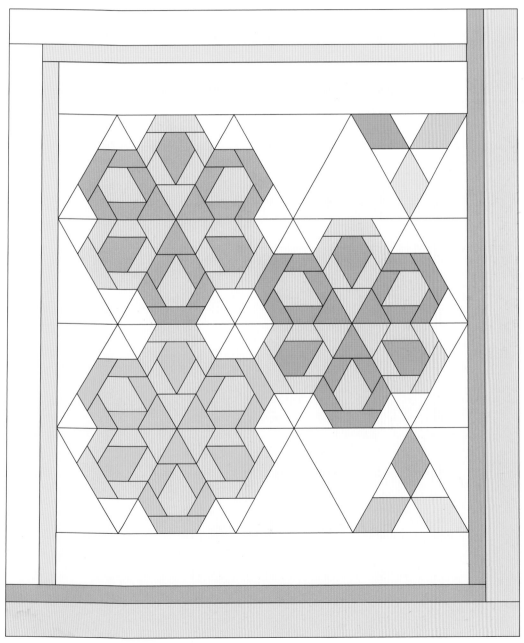

Quilt assembly

Finishing the Quilt

Layer the quilt top with the backing and batting. Baste.

Sue quilted *Apple Blossom Time* with a computerized design that has flowers in a hexagon arrangement. The petals have been stitched-in-the-ditch so that they would puff up and stand out. I then hand quilted inside the background flowers with Aurifil 12-weight thread. Even if you don't have time or don't want to do all of your quilting yourself, you can always add a personal touch with a little hand stitching.

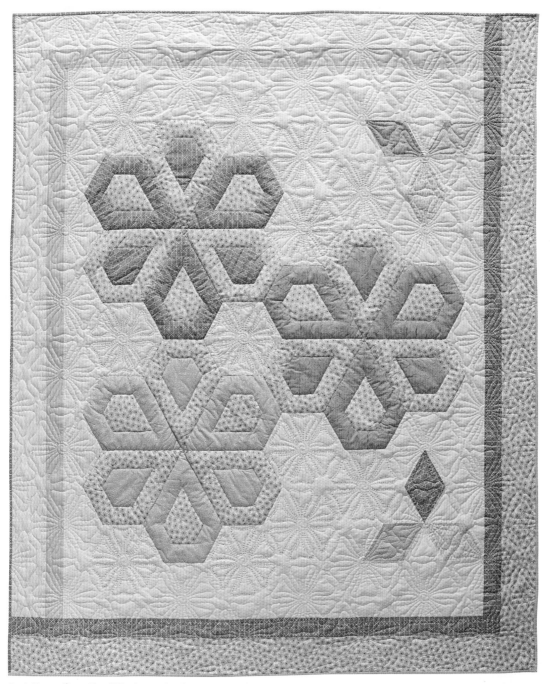

Apple Blossom Time, 61″ × 72½″, designed and pieced by Sheila Christensen, quilted by Sue Burnett and Sheila Christensen

LESSON SEVEN: 60° STRIP-PIECED QUILTS

STRIP-PIECING
BASICS

Strip piecing means joining strips of fabric before cutting. It is a way of speeding up the making of blocks. Add strip piecing to 60° patchwork, and you can make all sorts of quilts really quickly.

1. Remove selvages and line up strips at one end before sewing. This will mean you make the most of your fabrics. **FIG. A**

2. Sew with a ¼˝ seam and press the seams open. **FIG. B**

3. To cut strip sets, place them right side down and line the ruler up on the seams. **FIG. C**

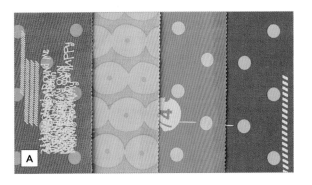

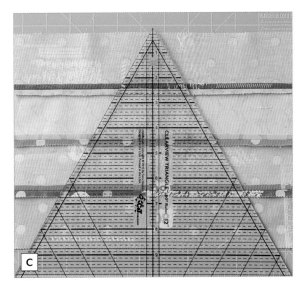

Murano

FINISHED BLOCK HEIGHT: 8″ · FINISHED QUILT: 65″ × 80½″

This is a perfect project for using your favorite bundle of 2½˝ strips. I used a precut 2½˝ strip bundle of Hey Dot by Zen Chic for Moda. These bright prints are really happy colors, and I love the sprinkling of white backgrounds in the collection. I think it gives the blocks the appearance of Venetian glass beads.

For the background, I chose a variety of low-volume prints. These background fabrics don't have to be monotone gray and white. Try creams with a tiny print or colorful prints on a white base. Alternatively, be dramatic and make a bold statement by using a dark background.

MATERIALS

Assorted feature fabrics: 40 strips 2½˝ × width of fabric for blocks (total approximately 3 yards with at least 41½˝ of usable width)

Assorted low-volume fabrics: ¼ yard *each* of 10 different low-volume fabrics (total 2½ yards) *or* use an even bigger variety of prints from your stash (the more the better!) for background

Binding: ⅝ yard

Backing: 5 yards

Batting: 73˝ × 89˝

CUTTING

For step-by-step cutting instructions, see 60° Triangle Basics (page 29). If you are using a straight ruler to cut triangles, see the note at the end of the cutting chart.

First, cut 40 strips 2½˝ × width of fabric from the feature fabrics (or use a precut roll).

Divide the strips into 10 sets of 4 strips each. Distribute the colors at random; there is no need to spend a lot of time planning. Sew strips together in their sets of 4. Make 10 strip sets measuring 8½˝ wide.

> **TIP** Cut the selvages sparingly off one end of each strip and line up these ends when joining. This will ensure you have enough to get seven triangles from each strip set.

SHAPE	CUT SIZE	FOR	FIRST, CUT STRIPS AND MAKE STRIP SETS:	SUBCUT FROM STRIPS:
Cut from *each* strip set:				
8˝ triangle	8½˝ tall, 10⅛˝ base	Blocks	Cut from each of 10 strip sets.	7 triangles (70 total)*
Assorted low-volume fabrics: Cut from *each* fabric:				
8˝ half-triangles	**Half-triangles:** 8½˝ tall, 5 5⁄16˝ base	Background	8½˝ × width of fabric	Place a mark ⅜˝ from one end of each strip. Cut a 60° angle from this mark to cut a half-triangle. Cut 6 full triangles* and then cut a second half-triangle (60 full triangles and 20 half-triangles total).
8˝ triangle	**Full triangles:** 8½˝ tall, 10⅛˝ base			
Binding				
8 strips 2½˝ × width of fabric				

*If using a straight ruler to cut the triangles, leave ⅜˝ between each cut along the strip so that you get triangles with blunt tips.

Construction

Seam allowances are ¼˝ unless otherwise noted. Press all seams open.

Quilt Assembly

1. Referring to the quilt assembly diagram, arrange the blocks in 10 rows with the background triangles and half-triangles.

2. Sew the triangles and blocks together in rows; then sew the rows together.

Quilt assembly

Finishing the Quilt

Quilt and bind the quilt as desired. A simple quilting pattern works really well in this quilt. Quilt vertical lines in the blocks and combine with horizontal lines in the background triangles.

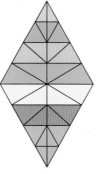

Alternative quilting suggestion for diamonds formed by two blocks

Alternative quilting suggestion for background

Murano, 65˝ × 80½˝, designed and pieced by Sheila Christensen, quilted by Sue Burnett

Pot of Gold

FINISHED BLOCK HEIGHT: 8˝ · **FINISHED QUILT:** 64½˝ × 74½˝

The legend is that a pot of gold is at the end of every rainbow. I don't know about any real gold in this quilt, but fabric is so much fun to play with that you might feel like you have found treasure!

I started with a roll of Tula Pink's True Colors for FreeSpirit Fabrics, and replaced some of the strips with other fabrics from her ranges. The large triangles are all Tula Pink fabrics.

Each of the rows is based on a color family, and the hexagon shapes created by the blocks help to make the rows merge together to give a smooth transition through the rainbow.

This quilt is arranged in columns rather than rows, and the half-triangles are placed at the top and bottom. Strip piecing is a great way to make this quilt quickly.

MATERIALS

Assorted fabrics in 5 color groups (blue, green, yellow, orange, and red):

1 strip 8½˝ × width of fabric *each of* 2 different prints (10 strips total)

1 strip 2½˝ × width of fabric *each of* 8 different prints (40 strips total for quilt) for pieced blocks (This project suits a precut 2½˝ strip bundle of rainbow colors.)

Deep violet: 1 strip 5⁵⁄₁₆˝ × width of fabric for bottom half-triangles

Magenta: 1 strip 5⁵⁄₁₆˝ × width of fabric for top half-triangles

Binding: ⅝ yard

Backing: 4¾ yards

Batting: 73˝ × 83˝

TIP Don't worry about keeping your fabrics in strictly separate groups. Mixing neighboring colors helps to blend the rows together. I used two of my blue/green prints in both the blue row and the green row.

CUTTING

For step-by-step cutting instructions, see 60° Triangle Basics (page 29). If you are using a straight ruler to cut triangles, see the note at the end of the cutting chart.

First, cut strips 2½˝ × width of fabric from the assorted 5 color groups (or use a precut bundle).

Divide the 2½˝ strips into 10 sets of 4 strips each, keeping similar colors together. Make 2 strip sets for each of the 5 color groupings. The strips sets should measure 8½˝ across.

SHAPE	CUT SIZE	FIRST, CUT STRIPS AND MAKE STRIP SETS:	SUBCUT FROM STRIPS:
		Cut from *each* strip set:	
Block A, 8˝ triangle Block B, 8˝ triangle	8½˝ tall, 10⅛˝ base	Cut from each of 10 strip sets.	6 triangles. Rotate the ruler as you cut so you have 3 each of Block A and Block B, with the colors in reverse order from each other.

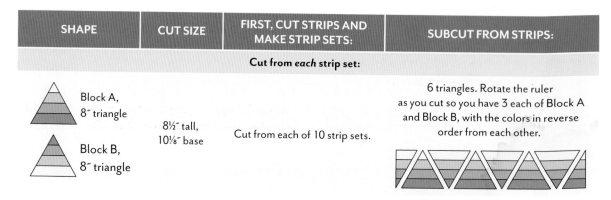

SHAPE	CUT SIZE	FIRST, CUT STRIPS AND MAKE STRIP SETS:	SUBCUT FROM STRIPS:
Assorted color groups (blue, green, yellow, orange, and red)			
8˝ triangle	8½˝ tall, 10⅛˝ base	From each 8½˝ strip (10 total)	6 triangles (60 total)*
Deep violet and magenta: Cut from *each* strip:			
8˝ half-triangles	9³⁄₁₆˝ × 5⁵⁄₁₆˝	1 strip 5⁵⁄₁₆˝ × width of fabric	8 half-triangles (16 total) from 4 rectangles (8 total) 5⁵⁄₁₆˝ × 9³⁄₁₆˝. Cut half the rectangles in one direction and the other half in the opposite.
Binding			
		8 strips 2½˝ × width of fabric	

*If using a straight ruler to cut the triangles, leave ⅜˝ between each cut along the strip so that you get triangles with blunt tips.

Construction

Seam allowances are ¼˝ unless otherwise noted.

Press all seams open.

Make the Hexagon Units

1. Arrange the triangles and Blocks A and B together to form hexagon units. Each color group will have 4 hexagon units.

TIP It is helpful to arrange the blocks in columns on a design wall, bed, or floor so you can keep track. The hexagon units are arranged so that the seams between the half-hexagons run vertically in the quilt. The half-triangles will be placed at the top and bottom.

2. Sew the blocks together to make half-hexagons. Pin the halves together, but don't sew them yet. Mix up the combinations of blocks and feature fabric triangles so that the same hexagon unit is not repeated.

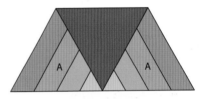

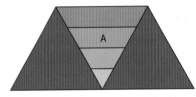

For each color grouping, make two pairs of half-hexagons with Block A, keeping the same whole triangle fabric in each pair.

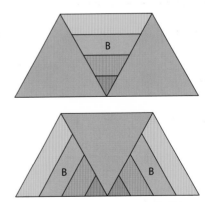

For each color grouping, make two pairs of half-hexagons with Block B, keeping the same whole triangle fabric in each pair.

Quilt Assembly

1. Referring to the quilt assembly diagram, arrange the hexagon units with the pinned half-hexagons aligned vertically in columns. Start with a half-triangle of magenta at the top.

> **NOTE** *For the orange and green color groups, split one hexagon unit to place a half-hexagon on the left side of the quilt and its partner on the right side during quilt assembly.*

2. Separate the half-hexagons and sew the blocks together in columns; then sew the columns together.

Quilt assembly

Finishing the Quilt

Quilt and bind the quilt as desired. Noeline used an edge-to-edge pattern in circles, which blends the blocks together well. If you enjoy free-motion stippling, you could do this as an allover pattern. An alternative is to follow the hexagon shapes as in the diagram (at right).

As the colors grade through the quilt, the binding color changes halfway along the sides.

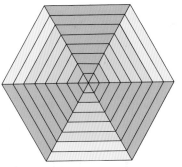

A great way to quilt concentric hexagons is to use the seam to travel from each hexagon to the next.

Pot of Gold, 64½˝ × 74½˝, designed and pieced by Sheila Christensen, quilted by Noeline Day

SKILL LEVEL: Beginner to intermediate

Slice of Heaven

FINISHED BLOCK HEIGHT: 12˝ · **FINISHED QUILT:** 70˝ × 74½˝

Fill up your bobbin and put on your favorite music. Strip piecing can be very meditative, and once you have joined the strips, the blocks will come together easily.

Choose a fabric you love and go from there. I started with the feature fabric from Cotton + Steel. It reminded me of the tree that sits just outside the window in my own little slice of heaven, under which I got married. On a sunny day, the yellow of the lemons looks so pretty against the blue sky.

For the background colors, I picked a fresh white to enhance the white lemon blossoms and then a muted gray. The gray works to soften the overall effect and calm down the busyness of the pattern. Once you have your feature fabric, you can pick other colors from the design to put into your quilt.

MATERIALS

Blue: 2⅛ yards for Block B and main border

Yellow: 1 yard for Block A and small border

White: 2 yards for Blocks A and B and side triangles

Gray: 2 yards for Blocks A and B and side triangles

Binding: ⅝ yard

Backing: 4¾ yards

Batting: 78″ × 83″

CUTTING

For step-by-step cutting instructions, see 60° Triangle Basics (page 29).

First, cut strips 2½″ × width of fabric from the following:

Blue: 9 strips   **Yellow:** 9 strips

White: 24 strips   **Gray:** 24 strips

Sew the 2½″ strips together to make the sets shown below. Press.

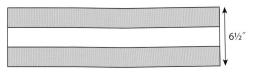

Strip set 1 (yellow/white/yellow): Make 3.

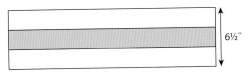

Strip set 2 (white/yellow/white): Make 3.

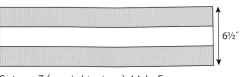

Strip set 3 (gray/white/gray): Make 5.

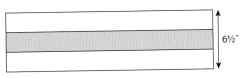

Strip set 4 (white/gray/white): Make 5.

Strip set 5 (blue/gray/blue): Make 3.

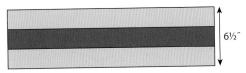

Strip set 6 (gray/blue/gray): Make 3.

SHAPE	CUT SIZE	FIRST, CUT STRIPS AND MAKE STRIP SETS:	SUBCUT FROM STRIPS:
Strip sets 1 and 2: Cut from *each*:			
6″ triangle	6½″ tall, 7¹³⁄₁₆″ base	Cut from strip sets.	20 triangles (40 total)
Strip sets 3 and 4: Cut from *each*:			
6″ triangle	6½″ tall, 7¹³⁄₁₆″ base	Cut from strip sets.	40 triangles (80 total)
Strip sets 5 and 6: Cut from *each*:			
6″ triangle	6½″ tall, 7¹³⁄₁₆″ base	Cut from strip sets.	15 triangles (30 total)
6″ half-triangles	4⅛″ × 6½″	Cut from strip sets.	6 rectangles (12 total) 4⅛″ × 6½″. Cut each in half diagonally, starting ⅜″ from the top and bottom edge. Cut 3 from top left to bottom right and 3 from top right to bottom left (24 half-triangles total). There will be 4 extra.
Yellow			
Inner border	1½″ strips	7 strips 1½″ × width of fabric	Join the strips; subcut 2 strips 1½″ × 56″ for the top and bottom inner borders and 2 strips 1½″ × 62½″ for the side inner borders.
Feature print			
Outer border	6½″ strips	7 strips 6½″ × width of fabric	Join the strips; subcut 2 strips 6½″ × 58″ for the top and bottom borders and 2 strips 6½″ × 74½″ for the side borders.

*If using a straight ruler to cut the triangles, leave ⅜″ between each cut along the strip so that you get triangles with blunt tips.

Construction

Seam allowances are ¼″ unless otherwise noted. Press all seams open.

Make the Blocks

1. Sew the triangle units together to make blocks. Press.

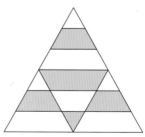

Block A: Make 20.

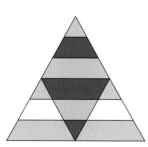

Block B: Make 15.

Block C: Make 5.

Block D: Make 5.

Quilt Assembly

1. Referring to the quilt assembly diagram, arrange the blocks in 5 rows.

2. Sew the blocks together in rows; then sew the rows together.

3. Add the inner borders—top and bottom first, then the sides.

4. Attach the outer borders—top and bottom first, then the sides.

Quilt assembly

Finishing the Quilt

Quilt and bind as desired. Although the quilt is constructed as a series of triangle blocks, it appears as if it is a series of diamonds once it is assembled. Sue emphasized this by quilting the colored diamonds with a different pattern than the gray-and-white diamonds.

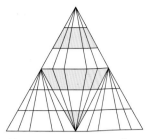

Alternative quilting suggestion

Slice of Heaven, 70˝ × 74½˝, designed and pieced by Sheila Christensen, quilted by Sue Burnett

LESSON EIGHT: DESIGN YOUR OWN 60° BLOCKS

When I first started designing 60° quilts, I spent a lot of time with graph paper and felt-tip pens, figuring out different blocks and looking at the patterns they would make when combined.

Using triangle graph paper (called isometric paper and available at any good art supply shop), you can draw your own 60° blocks and create unique quilt designs. Have fun exploring the possibilities.

60° TRIANGLE BLOCKS

I have found it easiest to make my blocks triangle-shaped. I think of triangles as the squares of 60° land.

Triangles fit together nicely, and rows can be finished off with half-triangles.

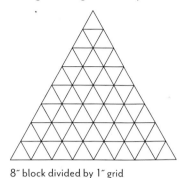

8″ block divided by 1″ grid

For this lesson, we will work with an 8″ finished triangle block and 2″ grid spacings.

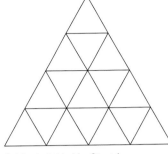

8″ block divided by 2″ grid

> **NOTE** *We are working with finished size here. For cutting instructions, see the lessons for each shape.*

Here I have colored in shapes to create a block which has 1 triangle 4″ finished and 12 triangles 2″ finished.

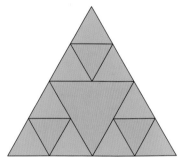

Block using all triangles

This block has 2 trapezoids 2 × 4 and 10 triangles 2″ finished.

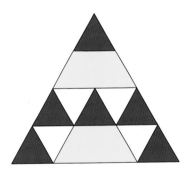

Here is another block using a 2″ diamond, a 2″ × 4″ right parallelogram, and a 2″ × 6″ right parallelogram, as well as 4 triangles 2″ finished height.

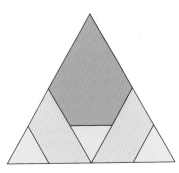

This block has a 4″ hexagon and 10 triangles 2″ finished height.

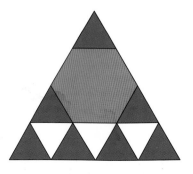

A 4″ jewel, 3 triangles 2″ finished, and 2 trapezoids 2 × 4 make this block.

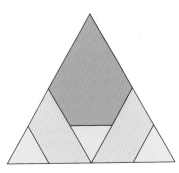

Try drawing these blocks on isometric paper and seeing what happens when you repeat them. Cut out the shapes and check that you can assemble the block with all straight seams. Then have a go at designing your own 60° blocks. Use the reference charts in each chapter to see how to cut each shape to the size needed. I look forward to seeing the results!

INDEX

RESOURCES

Longarm Quilting Designs for 60° Shapes

Sharon Perry   houseofcreations.biz

Your longarm quilting professional can purchase digital patterns from Sharon.

Longarm Quilting Services

Busy Bee Quilt Shop (Sue Burnett)   busybeequiltshop.co.nz

13 Kingsford Smith Street, Lyall Bay, Wellington 6022, New Zealand

Quilting Supplies, Patterns, Fabrics, and Classes

Quilters' Lane (Sheila Christensen)   quilterslane.co.nz

50a Queen Street, Masterton 5018, New Zealand

ABOUT THE AUTHOR

Sheila lives in Masterton, a small rural town in New Zealand, where she owns Quilters' Lane. She is originally from England and moved to New Zealand in 2002. She has also lived in Vevey, Switzerland; Utrecht in the Netherlands; North Carolina; and Florida.

As a teenager, Sheila learned to sew as a way of getting more clothes for less money. She learned mostly from her mum and sister. Her passion for quilting began later in life when she spotted a table runner class at the local quilt shop. After a few years of taking every class she could, she ended up buying the shop.

With a background in math and economics, Sheila has an eye for patterns and is fascinated by the endless possibilities in quilting. She has designed a precut puzzle mystery quilt every year since 2013—a program which is now sold worldwide. She loves sharing her knowledge by teaching in her shop and also at guilds and symposia.

Sheila is married to Carl, a Las Vegas native. Between them, they have six adult children and twelve grandchildren.

Photo by James Newton

Visit Sheila online and follow on social media!

Shop website: quilterslane.co.nz
(Visit her shop, Quilters' Lane, in New Zealand!)

Blog: mysteryquilter.com

Facebook: /mysteryquilter

Instragram: @mysteryquilter

Want even more creative content?

Go to ctpub.com/offer

& sign up to receive our gift to you!

Make it, snap it, share it *using #ctpublishing*